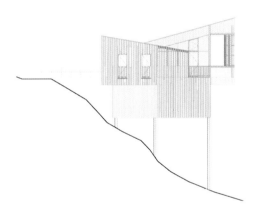

Editorial project:
2018 © booq publishing, S.L.
c/ Domènech, 7-9, 2° 1ª
08012 Barcelona, Spain
T: +34 93 268 80 88
www.booqpublishing.com

ISBN 978-84-9936-145-1 (EN)
ISBN 978-84-9936-108-6 (IT)

2018 French edition © Éditions du Layeur

ISBN 978-2-915126-56-3 [FR]

Editorial coordinator:
Claudia Martínez Alonso

Art director:
Mireia Casanovas Soley

Editor and layout:
David Andreu Bach

Translation:
Thinking Abroad [FR] [IT]

Printing in Spain

WDA (WILLIAM DUFF ARCHITECTS)
BIG RANCH ROAD
© Matthew Millman

FLANSBURG ARCHITECTS
JACOB'S PILLOW DANCE PERLES FAMILY STUDIO

© Robert Benson

Wood is one of the best materials for construction on account of its versatility. Among other benefits, its outstanding features are its great capacity as a thermal and acoustic insulator; its remarkable ecological character; warm appearance; luminosity, and comfort, as well as its pleasant texture and feel. For these reasons, architects and designers use this noble material, which offers infinite possibilities for exterior design and decoration. Today, the new criteria for sustainable housing planning benefit from an inexhaustible source of ideas based on products derived from this material. Furthermore, the great variety of available wood, and the fact that it is easy to recycle, facilitate the construction of masterful and varied designs. New ways of joining and fixing have been formulated thanks to modern technology.

The contact with nature that this material affords has successfully revitalized the use of wood in domestic architecture. In this sense, the clients who request these types of housing do so because they believe in the benefits that wood brings to their lives, satisfying their tastes, their requirements, and their individual lifestyles. This type of client requires energy efficiency, modern construction technologies, rapid assembly times and lower costs.

Wood Architecture Today selects 31 of the most relevant contemporary international architects who put this well-known medium into service in new and inspiring ways. A range of projects including homes, cabins, schools and chapels, all enhanced by the use of wood in both architectural and decorative settings, are featured in the pages of *Wood Architecture Today*.

Diverse architects and firms such as Tiago do Vale and Plano Humano Architects of Portugal, Lund Hagem of Norway, Landau + Kindelbacher of Germany, Lukkaroinen Architects of Finland have their most recent work featured in the pages of this inspiring collection.

Le bois est l'un des meilleurs matériaux de construction en raison de ses propriétés polyvalence. Parmi d'autres avantages, il se distingue par sa grande capacité à sa capacité d'isolation thermique et acoustique ; sa remarquable capacité écologique en matière d'isolation l'aspect chaleureux, la luminosité et le confort, ainsi que la qualité de l'éclairage texture et toucher agréables. Pour ces raisons, les architectes et les concepteurs utilisent ce matériau noble, qui offre des possibilités infinies en matière de design extérieur et d'aménagement. décoration. Aujourd'hui, les nouveaux critères de l'indemnité de planification de logement durable d'une source inépuisable d'idées basées sur des produits dérivés de ce produit matériel. De plus, la grande variété de bois disponible et le fait qu'il n'y a pas d'autres essences qu'il est facile de recycler, de faciliter la construction d'ouvrages d'art maîtrisés et variés dessins et modèles. De nouvelles méthodes d'assemblage et de fixation ont été formulées grâce à la technologie moderne.

Le contact avec la nature qu'offre ce matériau a permis de revitaliser avec succès l'utilisation du bois dans l'architecture domestique. En ce sens, les clients qui demander ces types de logement le font parce qu'ils croient en leurs avantages que le bois apporte à leur vie, en satisfaisant leurs goûts, leurs exigences, et leur mode de vie individuel. Ce type de client a besoin d'efficacité énergétique, des technologies de construction modernes, des temps de montage rapides et des coûts réduits.

Bois dans l'Architecture sélectionne 31 des architectes internationaux contemporains les plus importants qui mettent ce média bien connu au service d'une manière nouvelle et inspirante. Une gamme de projets comprenant des maisons, des cabanes, des écoles et des chapelles, tous mis en valeur par l'utilisation du bois dans des décors architecturaux et décoratifs, sont présentés dans les pages du *Bois dans l'Architecture*

Divers architectes et cabinets d'architectes tels que Tiago do Vale et Plano Humano Architects du Portugal, Lund Hagem de Norvège, Landau + Kindelbacher d'Allemagne, Lukkaroinen Architects de Finlande ont leurs travaux les plus récents dans les pages de cette collection inspirante.

Il legno è uno dei migliori materiali per l'edilizia grazie alle sue caratteristiche di versatilità. Tra gli altri vantaggi, le sue caratteristiche principali sono la sua grande capacità di isolamento termico e acustico; la sua notevole capacità ecologica carattere; aspetto caldo; luminosità e comfort, così come il suo aspetto caldo; luminosità e comfort, così come la sua texture e una sensazione piacevole al tatto. Per questi motivi, architetti e designer utilizzano questo nobile materiale, che offre infinite possibilità di design per esterni e di decorazione. Oggi, i nuovi criteri per la pianificazione edilizia sostenibile beneficio abitativo da un'inesauribile fonte inesauribile di idee basate su prodotti da essa derivati. Inoltre, la grande varietà di legno disponibile e il fatto che Inoltre, la grande varietà di legno disponibile, e il fatto che è facile da riciclare, facilitare la costruzione di opere magistrali e varie. Sono stati formulati nuovi modi di giunzione e fissaggio. Nuove modalità di giunzione e fissaggio sono state formulate grazie alla tecnologia moderna. Il contatto con la natura che questo materiale offre ha rivitalizzato con successo.

Il contatto con la natura che questo materiale offre ha rivitalizzato con successo l'uso del legno nell'architettura domestica. In questo senso, i clienti che richiedere questi tipi di alloggio lo fanno perché credono nei benefici che il legno porta alla loro vita, soddisfacendo i loro gusti, le loro esigenze, e il loro stile di vita individuale. Questo tipo di cliente richiede efficienza energetica, moderne tecnologie costruttive, tempi di montaggio rapidi e costi ridotti.

Legno Architettura Oggi seleziona 31 tra i più importanti architetti contemporanei internazionali che mettono a disposizione questo noto mezzo di comunicazione in modi nuovi e stimolanti. Una serie di progetti che includono case, cabine, scuole e cappelle, il tutto arricchito dall'uso del legno sia in ambito architettonico che decorativo, sono presenti nelle pagine di *Legno Architettura Oggi*.

Diversi architetti e studi come Tiago do Vale e Plano Humano Architects del Portogallo, Lund Hagem della Norvegia, Landau + Kindelbacher della Germania, Lukkaroinen Architects della Finlandia hanno i loro lavori più recenti sulle pagine di questa ispiratrice collezione.

2DM arquitectos is an architecture office based in Santiago de Chile, founded in 2014 by Daniel Díaz Miranda, who is an architect graduated in 2007 from the Universidad Técnica Federico Santa María. In 2007 he received the Federico Santa María Award, the highest award given by the university as the best graduate of his generation. In 2006 he completed undergraduate studies and a degree project in Italy at the Università Degli Studi di Ferrara. In 2014 he started 2DM architects, an architectural office devoted mainly to the development of private projects of different scale, in the residential, commercial and industrial fields.

Some of his works have been published in digital and printed architectural media in countries such as Spain, USA, France, Italy and Hong Kong.

2DM
ARQUITECTOS

WWW.2DM.CL

2DM arquitectos est un bureau d'architecte situé à Santiago de Chili. Il a été créé par Daniel Díaz Miranda, architecte diplômé en 2007 de l'Université technique Federico Santa María (Valparaiso, Chili). En 2007, il a reçu le prix Federico Santa María, la plus haute récompense remise par l'Université en tant que meilleur diplômé de sa promotion. En 2006, il a fait des études de premier cycle universitaire et un projet d'études en Italie, à l'Università Degli Studi di Ferrara. En 2014, il crée 2DM arquitectos, un cabinet d'architecte spécialisé dans le développement de divers projets privés dans les secteurs résidentiel, commercial et industriel.

Certains de ses travaux ont été publiés dans des médias numériques et classiques spécialisés dans l'architecture, de pays tels que l'Espagne, les États-Unis, la France, l'Italie et Hong-Kong.

2DM arquitectos è uno studio di architettura con sede a Santiago del Cile, fondato nel 2014 dall'architetto Daniel Díaz Miranda, laureatosi nel 2007 all'Università Tecnica Federico Santa María. Nel 2007 Daniel Díaz Miranda è insignito del premio Federico Santa María, il più alto riconoscimento assegnato dall'università al miglior laureato della sua classe. Nel 2006 è in Italia, per eseguire ricerche sull'istruzione pre-universitaria e la creazione di lauree presso l'Università Degli Studi di Ferrara. 2DM Arquitectos nasce nel 2014, ed è uno studio di architettura dedicato principalmente allo sviluppo di progetti privati di diversa natura, negli ambiti residenziale, commerciale e industriale.

Alcune delle sue opere sono apparse sulle pubblicazioni di architettura digitali e cartacee di paesi come Spagna, USA, Francia, Italia e Hong Kong.

2 CASAS EN PUERTECILLO

CASA RAPEL

WANKA LODGE

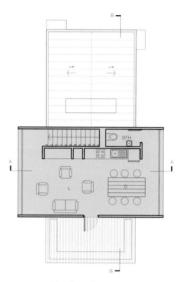

Third floor plan

The commission consisted of two waterfront houses, on a narrow piece of land, compressed by the sea and a cliff. Thus, the question arises immediately: how not to fall into the evident blatancy of the view to the sea, having it in front like an unavoidable scene with no mediating between sight and sea? The answer is to measure. A volume is then proposed that revolves in itself to receive the sea as a surprise, as a violent blow of sight, and a different perspective each and every time, as a sight that cannot be anticipated.

We can say that it is a work that achieves, not an immense, unique sea, but several, that of the northern rockery, Punta Puertecillo to the south, and so on. In this way, the two volumes that contain and tighten the volume appear: the sea and the cliff.

2 CASAS EN PUERTECILLO

© 2DM

Second floor plan

La commande comportait deux maisons de littoral, sur une parcelle étroite comprimée entre la mer et une falaise. La question s'est donc posée immédiatement : comment ne pas tomber dans l'évidence flagrante de la vue sur la mer, en l'ayant devant soi comme une scène inévitable sans médiation entre vision et mer ? La réponse est dans la mesure. Un volume est alors proposé qui tourne sur lui-même pour recevoir la mer comme une surprise, et une perspective différente à chaque fois en une vue qui ne peut pas être anticipée. Nous pouvons dire que c'est un ouvrage qui accomplit non pas une mer immense, unique, mais plusieurs, celle de la rocaille, au nord, celle de Punta Puertecillo, au Sud, etc. De cette façon, les deux volumes qui contiennent et compriment le module apparaissent : la mer et la falaise.

La commissione consisteva in due case fronte mare, su uno stretto appezzamento di terra tra il mare e una scogliera. Il problema si è presentato subito: come evitare di cadere nell'evidente petulanza di un panorama marino, avendolo di fronte come scenario inevitabile senza mediazione tra vista e mare? La risposta è stata la misura. È stato quindi proposto un volume che ruota su se stesso per accogliere il mare come una sorpresa, un impatto visivo violento ricevuto ogni volta da una prospettiva diversa, come qualcosa che non possa essere anticipato.

Si può dire che è l'opera riesce a regalare non un'unica distesa di acqua, ma tante e diverse: quella del giardino roccioso a nord, quella di Punta Puertecillo a sud, e così via. In questo modo, compaiono i due volumi che contengono e stringono la costruzione: il mare e la scogliera.

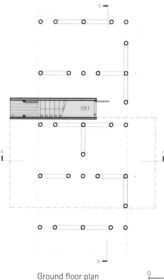

Ground floor plan

0   1m

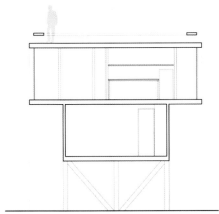

Section AA

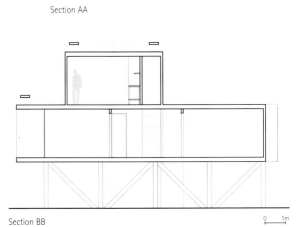

Section BB

0   1m

The commission consists of a summer house to be located in a rural area near Rapel Lake in a region of central Chile. The main characteristic that shapes the condition of the space is the extreme heat in summer times, a time that coincides with the greatest use of the house. In response to this requirement, the house responds with two basic strategies, it's own shade and ventilation. The house is thought of as a volume based on its own shadow, that is, the volume itself is capable of generating its own shadow through eaves at the ends of the house. A warehouse type volume, which in turn, achieves an appropriate height to move a mass of hot air away and renew it with cross ventilation. It is added to the strategy, to incorporate timber cladding to the roof to shade and microventilate the roof sheet. With the interior itself receiving minimal direct sunlight a cool environment for its occupants can be maintained.

CASA RAPEL
© 2DM

La commande était d'une maison d'été à implanter dans une zone rurale du centre du Chili près du lac Rapel. La caractéristique principale instruisant la condition de l'espace en est l'extrême chaleur estivale, période correspondant à l'utilisation la plus forte de la maison. Pour répondre à cette exigence, la maison offre deux stratégies de base : un ombrage et une aération qu'elle génère elle-même. Cette habitation est pensée comme un volume basé sur sa propre ombre, en ce que le volume-même est capable de générer sa propre ombre par le biais de débords de toit à chacune de ses extrémités. Un volume rappelant celui d'un entrepôt qui, à son tour, atteint une hauteur suffisante pour déplacer une masse d'air chaud et la renouveler à l'aide d'une aération transversale. En plus de cette stratégie, l'incorporation d'un bardage de bois à la toiture pour faire de l'ombre à la couverture et la micro-ventiler. L'intérieur-même ne recevant que peu de lumière directe, il est possible d'y maintenir un environnement frais pour ses occupants.

La commissione consiste in una casa per le vacanze, da costruire su un'area rurale vicino al Lago Rapel, in una regione centrale del Cile. La caratteristica principale da tenere in considerazione per modulare lo spazio è l'eccessiva calura estiva, periodo di maggiore utilizzo della casa. In risposta a questo requisito, la casa mette in campo due strategie di base: l'ombra e la ventilazione. La casa viene pensata come un volume che si basi sulla propria ombra; il volume stesso, cioè, è capace di generare la propria ombra grazie alle tettoie poste ai suoi estremi. Un volume che rassomiglia a un magazzino, che raggiunga un'altezza adeguata per spostare le masse d'aria calda e favorire la ventilazione incrociata. Ciò si aggiunge alla strategia di integrare un rivestimento in legno nel tetto per dare ombra e ventilare la copertura. L'ambiente interno si mantiene fresco per gli abitanti riducendo al minimo l'ingresso della luce solare diretta.

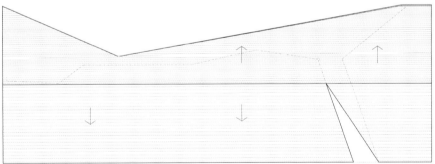

Roof plan

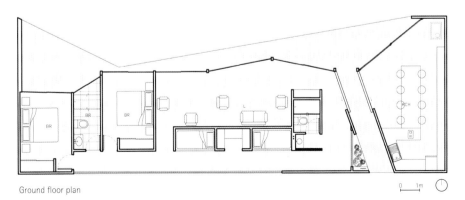

Ground floor plan

0   1m

The project consisted in the design of a series of cabins for 2 people in a reduced size lot which forced to make privacy the main target to consider in the design process. As the number of cabins increased, more privacy was required. This is how each unit is conceived as an interior, as a continuous element that becomes floor, wall or sky. This operation creates double walls generating an acoustic protection towards the nearest neighbors. In this way the fold begins its closing towards its more opaque centre making it appear only with a bouncing light, praising the requiered intimacy.

Site plan

WANKA LODGE
© 2DM

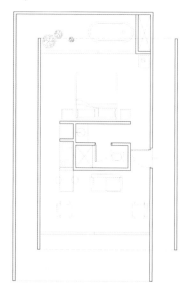

Ground floor plan   0   1m

Sa mission consistait à concevoir une série de cabanes pour 2 personnes dans un lot d'une taille assez réduite, obligeant à faire de l'intimité le principal facteur à prendre en considération lors de la phase de conception. Plus le nombre de cabanes augmentait, plus cela demandait de l'intimité, car la proximité se faisait ressentir. Chaque cabane est proposée comme un intérieur à partir d'une opération de rabattement et de déploiement d'un élément continu qui se transforme en appartement, mur ou plafond. Cette opération offre de façon appropriée des doubles murs créant ainsi un écran sonore vers les voisins les plus proches. De cette manière, le rabattement commence à se refermer vers son centre le plus opaque en faisant apparaître uniquement une lumière qui met en valeur l'intimité requise.

L'incarico prevedeva la progettazione di una serie di bungalow per 2 persone su un lotto piccolo abbastanza da fare della privacy l'aspetto più importante da tenere in considerazione durante il processo. Più aumentava il numero dei bungalow, più cresceva l'attenzione alla privacy, riducendosi la distanza tra una struttura e l'altra. Ecco come ogni bungalow viene proposto, con un interno che scaturisce dall'azione di ripiegatura di un elemento continuo, che diventa di volta in volta pavimento, parete, soffitto. Opportunamente, l'operazione genera muri doppi utili a promuovere l'isolamento acustico tra bungalow contigui. È così che era la ripiegatura procede fino al proprio nucleo più opaco, evocandolo con la sola luce di rimbalzo che elogia l'intimità desiderata.

AchterboschZantman International is involved in regional projects as well as projects all over the world. Within major and integral design tasks we think gathering a wide scope of experience and intellect is a necessity. This leads to professionalism and enhancing the quality of architecture and urbanism service. Transposition in the end-user and respecting the context makes a difference in our work. Quality of space is about the value of the living environment, on a specific location at a certain moment in time. The quality of space is hidden in buildings, in the village, in the city and landscape. Quality emerges when vision, creativity, craftsmanship and decisiveness meets. In the design process AchterboschZantman architects uses a critical attitude concerning the usual. Integral thinking and architectonic intuition will lead to original, inventive and sometimes experimental designs.

© Laurens Aaij

ACHTERBOSCHZANTMAN INTERNATIONAL

WWW.ACHTERBOSCHZANTMAN.NL

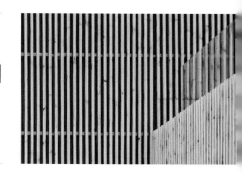

AchterboschZantman International est impliqué dans des projets au niveau régional ainsi que dans le monde entier. Pour des missions de design majeures et intégrales, nous pensons qu'il est nécessaire de réunir un large éventail d'expérience et de qualités intellectuelles. Cela mène au professionnalisme et met en valeur la qualité de l'architecture et du service d'urbanisme. S'imaginer à la place de l'utilisateur et respecter le contexte font une grande différence dans notre travail. La qualité de l'espace est dissimulée dans les bâtiments, dans le village, la ville et le paysage. Celle-ci émerge lorsque la vision, la créativité, le savoir-faire artisanal et l'esprit de décision convergent. Dans le processus de design les architectes d'AchterboschZantman ont une attitude critique vis-à-vis de la chose habituelle. Pensée intégrale et intuition architectonique sont nécessaires pour mener à des designs originaux, inventifs et parfois expérimentaux.

Lo studio AchterboschZantman International è impegnato in progetti sia regionali che internazionali. Nell'ambito di impegni progettuali di fondamentale importanza, crediamo che radunare un'ampia varietà di competenze e intelligenze sia una necessità. Un approccio del genere porta professionalità ed esalta la qualità dell'architettura e dell'urbanistica. Mettersi nei panni dell'utente finale e rispettare il contesto sono fattori che fanno la differenza, nel nostro lavoro. La qualità dello spazio riguarda il valore dell'ambiente di vita in un luogo specifico, in un determinato momento. La qualità si nasconde negli edifici, nei piccoli centri, nelle grandi città e nel paesaggio. La qualità emerge quando visione, creatività, abilità e determinazione si incontrano. Nelle fasi della progettazione, gli architetti di AchterboschZantman si pongono davanti all'usuale con un approccio critico. Il pensiero integrale e l'intuizione architettonica porteranno a progetti originali, ricchi di inventiva e qualche volta sperimentali.

EE RESIDENCE

SNEEK BRIDGE
First Prize, Wood innovation prize 2010,
OAK (Onix Achterbos Kunstwerken)

MEIJIE MOUNTAIN HOTSPRING RESORT
First prize, WAN AWARDS, resort complex award
Finalist, World Architecture Festival 2018
Continental Diamond award, annual tourist resort hotel

Hidden in the outskirts of Leeuwarden at the former river EE this energy-neutral house is overlooking the open Frisian landscape. The transitions of the open landscape into the urban area gave directions to the design. The closed north side provides privacy in contrast to the private south side where the house opens up and connects to the garden. The south orientation with the large porch ensures a delicate balance between natural cooling in the summer and warmth of the low standing sun in the winter. A multi-shaped roof provided with thatch and wood meanders over the substructure and provides space for the program and an outdoor terrace. The roof follows function, light, air and important lines of sight, and covers the house like a blanket. The location-specific and mostly ecological materials are inspired by the agricultural environment and remind us of the typical Frisian farm barns. The house is constructed with attention to forgotten craftsmanship in wood constructions.

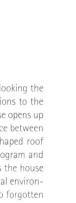

Site plan

EE RESIDENCE

© Ronald Zijlstra

Cachée dans les faubourgs de Leeuwarden sur l'EE, ancienne rivière, cette maison neutre en énergie donne sur le paysage ouvert de la Frise. Le passage de ce paysage ouvert à la zone urbaine a orienté le design. Le côté nord, fermé, procure de l'intimité en contraste avec le côté sud, privé, sur lequel la maison s'ouvre et communique avec le jardin. L'orientation vers le sud avec le grand porche garantit un équilibre délicat entre la climatisation naturelle en été et la chaleur du soleil rasant de l'hiver. Un toit aux diverses formes couvert de chaume et de bois ondule sur la charpente et procure de l'espace pour la programmation du bâtiment et une terrasse extérieure. Cette couverture suit ses fonctions, la lumière, l'air et des lignes de perspectives importantes ; il enveloppe la maison à la manière d'une couverture. Les matériaux spécifiques à la région et majoritairement écologiques sont inspirés par l'environnement agricole et nous rappellent les granges frisonnes typiques. Cette maison est construite avec le souci des savoir-faire oubliés des constructions en bois.

Lo studio AchterboschZantman International è impegnato in progetti sia regionali che internazionali. Nell'ambito di impegni progettuali di fondamentale importanza, crediamo che radunare un'ampia varietà di competenze e intelligenze sia una necessità. Un approccio del genere porta professionalità ed esalta la qualità dell'architettura e dell'urbanistica. Mettersi nei panni dell'utente finale e rispettare il contesto sono fattori che fanno la differenza, nel nostro lavoro. La qualità dello spazio riguarda il valore dell'ambiente di vita in un luogo specifico, in un determinato momento. La qualità si nasconde negli edifici, nei piccoli centri, nelle grandi città e nel paesaggio. La qualità emerge quando visione, creatività, abilità e determinazione si incontrano. Nelle fasi della progettazione, gli architetti di AchterboschZantman si pongono davanti all'usuale con un approccio critico. Il pensiero integrale e l'intuizione architettonica porteranno a progetti originali, ricchi di inventiva e qualche volta sperimentali.

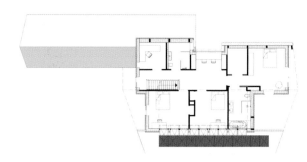

First floor plan

Ground floor plan

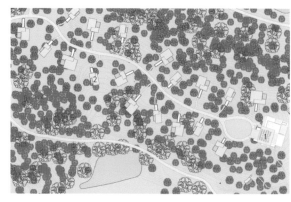

Site plan

Meijie Mountain Hotspring Resort is located in Liyang, China. The resort hides itself in the city's most beautiful Longtan Forest, which is lying between Tianmu Lake and Nanshan Bamboo. The elegant resort is a benchmark for sustainable eco design. The Meijie Mountain Hotspring Resort integrates four ecological elements: forest, tree houses, hot spring and mountains. The resort is suitable for ecological and recreational tourism as well for commercial gatherings. To minimize the ecological footprint the 31 houses are cleverly setup on poles in the lush treetops of the Nanshan jungle. They are constructed with local natural materials such as bamboo and local wood. The resort's hot springs are streaming along the hillsides and lying on the meadow, with the sky and mountains reflecting in it. The spring water is clear and mild. The interior and exterior design are unified, in order to ensure a perfect final result, all the details including furniture and light are all chosen by Achterboschzantman architect.

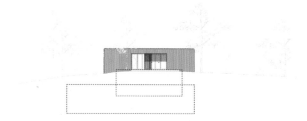

MEIJIE MOUNTAIN HOTSPRING RESORT

© Anna de Leeuw

Meijie Mountain Hotspring Resort est situé à Liyang, en Chine. Cette station se cache dans la plus magnifique forêt de la ville, Longtan Forest, qui se tient entre le lac Tianmu et Nanshan Bamboo. Cet élégant lieu de villégiature est une référence en matière de design écologique durable. Il intègre quatre éléments écologiques : la forêt, les maisons dans les arbres, la source d'eau chaude et les montagnes. Il est adapté au tourisme vert et aux activités récréotouristiques ainsi qu'aux réunions commerciales. Pour minimiser leur empreinte écologique, les 31 maisons sont judicieusement installées sur pilotis dans la couronne d'arbres luxuriante de la jungle de Nanshan. Elles sont construites avec des matériaux naturels locaux tels que le bambou et les essences de bois locales. Les sources d'eau chaude de la station ruissellent le long des flancs de la colline et se répandent sur la prairie, le ciel et les montagnes s'y reflétant. L'eau de source y est claire et douce. Le design de l'intérieur et de l'extérieur sont harmonisés afin de garantir un résultat final parfait, tous les détails comprenant le mobilier et l'éclairage sont choisis par Achterboschzantman architects.

Il Meijie Mountain Hotspring Resort si trova a Liyang, Cina. Il resort si erge protetto dalla foresta più bella dei dintorni, la Foresta Longtan, estesa tra il Lago Tianmu e Nanshan Bamboo. L'elegante resort è un punto di riferimento in materia di progettazione ecosostenibile. Il Meijie Mountain Hotspring Resort integra quattro elementi naturali: la foresta, le case sugli alberi, le sorgenti termali e le montagne. Il resort è adatto al turismo ecologico e da diporto, ma anche per le riunioni di carattere commerciale. Per ridurre al minimo l'impatto ambientale, le 31 case poggiano su pali inseriti nelle rigogliose cime degli alberi della foresta di Nanshan. I materiali da costruzione sono locali e naturali: bambù e legno del posto. Le sorgenti termali scorrono lungo i fianchi delle colline per raccogliersi nei prati, dove riflettono il cielo e le montagne. L'acqua è limpida e tiepida. Il design interno e quello esterno sono uniformi, per garantire un risultato finale perfetto. Tutti i dettagli, inclusi l'arredamento e l'illuminazione sono scelti da Achterboschzantman architetti.

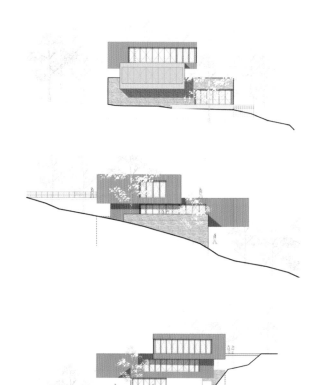

Club House elevations

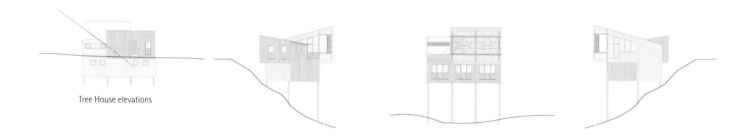

Tree House elevations

In collaboration with Onix under the combined name of OAK we designed a road bridge for a municipality that wishes to establish a new recognizable city marker-icon along the A7 motorway in Sneek. The Department of Public Works stated that it wants to use more wood in its constructions. For the design team, it is the challenge to realize a bridge in a responsible and sustainable way, and to capitalize on the latest innovations in wood construction. The contours call to mind the traditional roof shape of the traditional farm houses in Friesland, and evokes reminiscences of the buildings that are abundantly present in the old city. The wooden beams reflect the shipbuilding industry, with Sneek as a well known water recreation city in the Netherlands. All these aspects led to the first uncovered wooden bridge in the heaviest load class of 60. This bridge is not only a novelty for the Netherlands but also for countries such as Canada, Norway and Switzerland where the covered bridge is a well- known feature.

SNEEK BRIDGE

© Peter de Kan

En collaboration avec Onix sous le nom combiné d'OAK, nous avons conçu un pont routier pour une municipalité qui souhaite établir un nouveau symbole reconnaissable de la ville le long de l'autoroute A7 à Sneek. Le département des travaux publics a spécifié qu'il voulait utiliser davantage de bois dans ses constructions. Pour l'équipe de design, c'est un défi de réaliser un pont d'une manière responsable et durable, et de tirer profit des dernières innovations de la construction en bois. Les contours évoquent la forme de toiture typique des fermes traditionnelles de la Frise, et rappellent les bâtiments qui sont présents en abondance dans la vieille ville. Les poutres en bois reflètent l'industrie navale, Sneek étant une ville connue dans les Pays-Bas pour ses activités nautiques. Tous ces aspects ont mené au premier pont découvert en bois avec une charge pouvant atteindre 60 tonnes. Ce pont n'est pas seulement une nouveauté pour les Pays-Bas mais aussi pour des pays tels que le Canada, la Norvège et la Suisse où le pont couvert est chose courante.

In collaborazione con Onix sotto la denominazione combinata di OAK, abbiamo progettato un ponte stradale lungo l'autostrada A7 di Sneek, per una città desiderosa di consegnare la propria immagine a una nuova icona. Il Dipartimento dei Lavori Pubblici aveva dichiarato la volontà di utilizzare più legno nelle costruzioni. Per il team di progettazione, la sfida è stata realizzare un ponte in modo responsabile e sostenibile, facendo tesoro delle più recenti innovazioni in materia di costruzioni in legno. Il profilo richiama alla mente la tradizionale forma dei tetti delle fattorie in Frisia, ed evoca reminiscenze delle costruzioni ancora presenti in abbondanza nella città vecchia. Le travi in legno sono un'eco dell'industria cantieristica navale, essendo Sneek nota in tutti i Paesi Bassi per le attività nautiche da diporto. Tutti questi aspetti hanno portato alla costruzione del primo ponte scoperto in legno, adatto anche a veicoli con classe di carico più elevata (60 t). Il ponte rappresenta una novità non soltanto per i Paesi Bassi, ma anche per paesi come il Canada, la Norvegia e la Svizzera, dove il concetto di ponte coperto è ben noto.

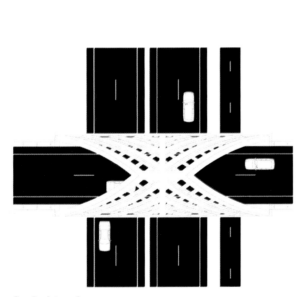

Overview intersection

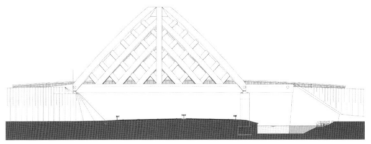

Side view east side

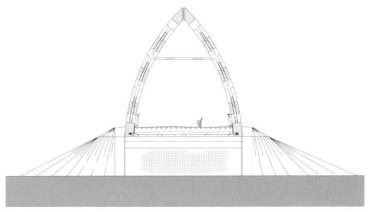

Cross section

Our aim at AIX is to create architecture that makes a difference and creates a better society. We design high-quality contemporary architecture, taking careful account of existing buildings. Our aim is to form spatial experiences where function and beauty intermingle, reinforcing one another: spaces that evoke feelings, change with the times and provide the best setting for people to live and to interact. With our wide variety of expertise our team can work together to find the best solution for every individual project. We operate city planning and residential properties, cultural environment and restoration, commercial, public and educational premises, theater technology, interior and lighting design. Wood constructions is one of our special areas of expertise.

AIX
ARKITEKTER

WWW.AIX.SE

Notre objectif, chez AIX, est de créer une architecture qui fait la différence et crée une société meilleure. Nous concevons une architecture contemporaine de haute qualité, en tenant le plus grand compte des constructions d'origine. Nous visons à former des expériences spatiales là où fonctionnalité et beauté se rejoignent, se renforçant l'une l'autre : des espaces qui évoquent des sentiments, changent avec le temps et offrent le meilleur cadre de vie et d'interaction pour leurs occupants.
Avec notre large variété de compétences, notre équipe peut collaborer pour trouver la meilleure solution pour chaque projet individuel. Nous intervenons dans la planification urbaine et la propriété résidentielle, l'environnement culturel et la restauration, les locaux commerciaux, publics et éducatifs, la technologie théâtrale, le design d'intérieur et la conception d'éclairage.

Il nostro scopo come AIX è creare un'architettura che faccia la differenza e generi una società migliore. Progettiamo architettura contemporanea di alta qualità, tenendo in grande considerazione gli edifici esistenti. Vogliamo dare vita a esperienze spaziali all'interno delle quali funzionalità e bellezza si mescolino rafforzandosi a vicenda: spazi che evochino sensazioni, che cambino nel tempo e offrano lo scenario migliore per vivere e interagire.
Grazie alla nutrita diversità di competenze, il nostro team è in grado di collaborare alla ricerca della soluzione migliore per ogni singolo progetto. Operiamo nei seguenti campi: pianificazione urbana e immobili residenziali, ambiente culturale e recupero, locali commerciali, pubblici e dati all'istruzione, tecnologia teatrale, design di interni e dell'illuminazione. Le costruzioni in legno costituiscono una delle nostre aree specialistiche di competenza.

KATA FARM

DRESSYRHALLEN

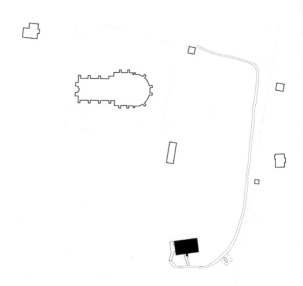

Site plan

When archaeologists excavated a hill near Varnhem monastery church, they found the ruins of one of Sweden's oldest churches. A private yard church from the Viking era, ruled by a woman named Kata. The church crypt is perhaps the oldest preserved room in Sweden. Our task was to protect its foundations and graves while making its history accessible to all visitors. The shelter consists of a simple triangular roof structure. As the visitor enters the space, its unearthed underside unfolds. The wooden architecture is meant to bring warmth into the space while the detailing is visible and tactile to all senses. There are two windows in the room. One small vertical slot in the eastern gable overlooking both chancel and crypt of the original church. The other window makes visible connection to the Varnhem church at distance. Underground below the church is were Katas grave still contains her remains, visible through a glass part of the floor. A protective chamber was built around her burial to prolong and restore its dignity.

KATA FARM

© Antonius van Arkel

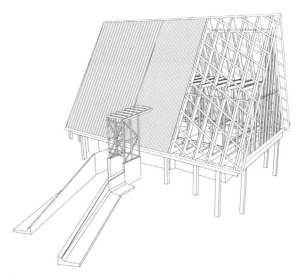

Construction, perspective

Lorsque des archéologues ont excavé une colline près du monastère de Varnhem, ils ont trouvé les ruines d'une des plus anciennes églises de Suède. Un enclos paroissial privé de l'époque viking, dirigé par une femme nommée Kata. La crypte de cette église est peut-être la plus ancienne salle conservée de Suède. Notre tâche était de protéger ses fondations et ses tombes tout en rendant son histoire accessible à tous les visiteurs. L'abri consiste en une structure de toit triangulaire simple. À mesure que le visiteur pénètre dans l'espace, la partie inférieure mise au jour se révèle. L'architecture en bois sert à apporter de la chaleur à l'espace et les détails de construction sont visibles et font appel à tous les sens. Cette pièce est percée de deux fenêtres. L'une, fente verticale pratiquée sur le pignon, donne à la fois sur le chœur et la crypte de l'église d'origine. L'autre rend visible le lien avec l'église de Varnem au loin. Au-dessous de l'église, au sous-sol, la tombe de Katas, visible au travers d'une partie vitrée du sol, contient toujours sa dépouille. Une chambre de protection a été construite autour de sa sépulture pour lui rendre sa dignité et la prolonger.

Durante alcuni scavi presso una collina vicino alla chiesa del monastero di Varnhem, gli archeologi rinvenirono le rovine di una delle più antiche chiede della Svezia. Una cappella privata risalente all'epoca dei Vichinghi, guidata da una donna chiamata Kata. La cripta è forse la più antica camera meglio conservata di tutta la Svezia. Il nostro compito è stato quello di proteggerne le fondamenta, rendendo al contempo la sua storia accessibile ai visitatori. Il ricovero è formato da una struttura semplice, con tetto triangolare. Entrando, il visitatore può scoprire la sua parte inferiore riportata alla luce. L'architettura in legno vuole dare calore allo spazio, rendendo i dettagli visibili e accessibili a tutti i sensi. Nella stanza ci sono due finestre. Una stretta fessura nel timpano a est, che guarda sul presbiterio e la cripta della chiesa originale. L'altra finestra rende visibile da lontano il collegamento alla chiesa di Varnhem. Nei sotterranei della chiesa, la tomba di Kata contiene ancora i suoi resti, ed è visibile attraverso una lastra di vetro nella pavimentazione. Per prolungare e salvaguardarne la dignità, è stata costruita una camera di protezione attorno al sepolcro.

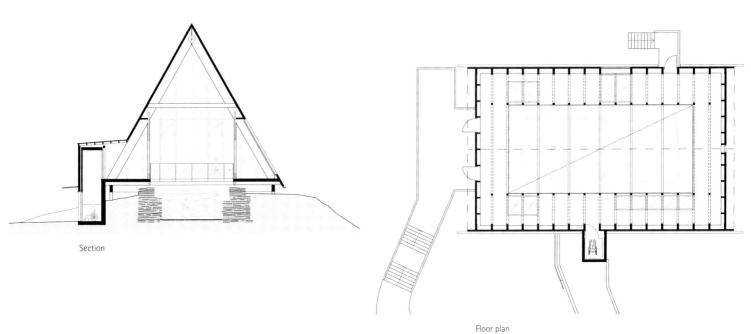

Section

Floor plan

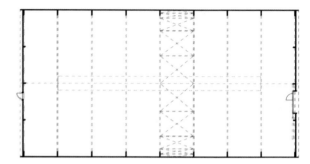

Floor plan

The Swedish Police Force needed a new training facility. A simple, rational structure —in a sensitive cultural-historical environment. While being cost effective, the demand on building expression was high, one that needed to offer high caliber architecture most suitable for Rosersberg Palace.

The solution: making the best out of a modern yet noble material: cross laminated timber slabs. The 1.2 x 11 m elements were used as would an upside-down clinker boat. The capacity to absorb the load of the 5.8 m. span without secondary trusses was met by overlapping these slabs creating exceptional shear strength. In this way full-length slabs needed only one truss support. Added to this, extremely time efficient construction through minimal number of elements achieved a straight forward, sophisticated expression. In the end the form indeed stood out amongst the older structures while the architecture lives up to the same principles: rationality, robustness and a functional beauty.

DRESSYRHALLEN

© Peder Lindbom

La police suédoise avait besoin de nouveaux locaux d'entraînement. Une structure simple, rationnelle - dans un environnement culturel et historique sensible. Tout en étant économiquement rentable, l'exigence de caractère pour le bâtiment était élevée, demandant une architecture du niveau de celle du Palais de Rosersberg. La solution : tirer le meilleur parti d'un matériau moderne et noble : des lames de bois stratifié-croisé. Les éléments de 1,2 x 11 m ont été utilisés comme pour une embarcation à clin renversée. La capacité d'absorption de la charge des 5.8 m de portée sans avoir recours à des fermes secondaires a été obtenue par le chevauchement de ces lames, créant une résistance en cisaillement exceptionnelle. Ainsi les lames de bois n'ont nécessité qu'un seul soutien supplémentaire. Qui plus est, cette construction très efficace en termes de temps de par l'utilisation d'un nombre limité d'éléments est parvenue à produire une expression directe, sophistiquée. Finalement cette forme s'est démarquée parmi des structures plus anciennes tandis que son architecture respecte les mêmes principes : la rationalité, la robustesse et une beauté fonctionnelle.

Le Forze di polizia svedesi avevano bisogno di un nuovo centro di addestramento. Una struttura semplice, razionale, immersa in un ambiente dal forte carattere storico-culturale. Il progetto, per quanto efficiente in termini di costi, doveva essere all'altezza del carattere architettonico del Palazzo di Rosersberg. La soluzione: trarre il meglio da un materiale moderno ma nobile: lastre di legno lamellare a strati incrociati. Gli elementi da 1,2 x 11 m sono stati assemblati come per una barca a clinker sottosopra. La capacità di assorbimento del carico della campata da 5,8 m, senza l'aiuto di travi secondarie è stata raggiunta sovrapponendo le lastre e generando un'eccezionale resistenza al taglio. In questo modo, le lastre a lunghezza intera hanno necessitato una sola trave di supporto. Si aggiunga a questo che la costruzione, la cui durata nel tempo è stata assicurata dall'impiego di un numero minimo di elementi, ha raggiunto un carattere diretto e sofisticato. In definitiva, la forma spicca tra le altre strutture più antiche, mentre l'architettura si nutre degli stessi principi: razionalità, robustezza e bellezza funzionale.

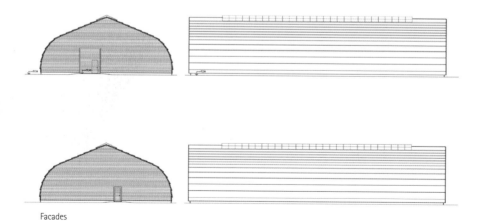

Facades

Arthur W. Andersson and F. Christian Wise founded Andersson·Wise Architects in 2001 following a 15-year collaboration with the late Charles W. Moore. Moore is recognized as having been one of this century's greatest architects; his work, writings, and teachings have profoundly influenced the course of architecture worldwide. Andersson·Wise has become a collaborative of 20 architects and designers dedicated to excellence in public and private architectural design and interiors. Arthur Andersson has practiced architecture throughout the US since 1980. He was educated at the Univ. of Kansas and the Univ. of London, and has taught design at Tulane University, The University of Texas at Austin, and the University of Houston. Chris Wise's work with Andersson and Moore began in 1985, after an internship with Venturi, Rauch, Scott Brown in Philadelphia, PA. He was educated at the University of Texas and received a Master of Design Studies from Harvard University and has taught design at the University of Texas.

ANDERSSON·WISE

WWW.ANDERSSONWISE.COM

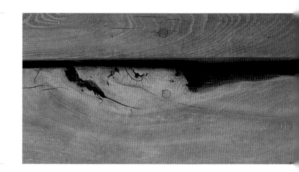

Arthur W. Andersson et F. Christian Wise ont fondé Andersson·Wise Architects en 2001, à la suite de 15 ans de collaboration avec feu Charles W. Moore. Moore est reconnu pour avoir été l'un des architectes les plus importants de ce siècle ; ses travaux, ses écrits, et ses enseignements ont profondément influencé le cours de l'architecture dans le monde entier. Andersson Wise est devenu un partenariat collaboratif de 20 architectes et designers engagés pour l'excellence dans le design architectural et d'intérieur public et privé. Arthur Andersson pratique l'architecture à travers les États-Unis depuis 1980. Il a étudié à l'Université du Kansas et l'Université de Londres, et a enseigné le design à l'Université Tulane, l'Université du Texas à Austin et l'Université de Houston. Le travail de Chris Wise avec Andersson et Moore a commencé en 1985, après un stage avec Venturi, Rauch, Scott Brown à Philadephie, PA. Il a étudié à l'Université du Texas et a reçu un Mastère en Design Studies d'Harvard et enseigné le design à l'Université du Texas.

Arthur W. Andersson e F. Christian Wise hanno fondato la Andersson·Wise Architects nel 2001, dopo una collaborazione durata 15 anni con il compianto Charles W. Moore. La fama di Moore come uno dei più grandi architetti del secolo scorso è riconosciuta; le sue opere, i suoi scritti e insegnamenti hanno inciso profondamente sul corso dell'architettura mondiale. Lo studio Andersson·Wise è diventato un laboratorio con 20 architetti e designer devoti all'eccellenza nei campi del design architettonico e di interni sia pubblico che privato. Arthur Andersson si occupa di architettura in tutti gli Stati Uniti fin dal 1980. Ha studiato all'Univ. del Kansas e all'Univ. di Londra, ha insegnato progettazione presso l'Univ. Tulane, l'Univ. del Texas ad Austin e l'Univ. di Houston. Chris Wise comincia a lavorare con Andersson and Moore nel 1985, dopo un tirocinio con Venturi, Rauch, Scott Brown a Filadelfia, Pennsylvania. Ha studiato all'Univ. del Texas e superato un Master of Design Studies all'Univ. di Harvard. Ha insegnato progettazione all'Univ. del Texas.

TOWER HOUSE

CABIN ON FLATHEAD LAKE

BUNNY RUN BOAT DOCK

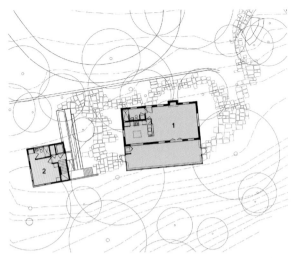

1. Renovated lodge
2. New tower

There are small limestone cabins from the 1930s located along Lake Travis, the longest of the Highland Lakes that terrace the hill country west of Austin, and they are used primarily in the summer. One such cabin sits on a slope rising from the water under a canopy of native oaks and cedars. It had one large room, a little sleeping room, a kitchen, and a porch facing the water. Our client requested two additional bedrooms with baths and a living area for larger groups to gather. We chose to locate the new sleeping quarters in a separate tower. Two small bedrooms occupy the first and second floors. Above, a third level terrace opens to a panorama of the lake and distant rolling hills. On this terrace, some thirty feet above the ground, even the hottest summer afternoon can be enjoyed under a roof open to the prevailing breezes blowing in from the lake. The original stone cabin is now juxtaposed with a vertical tower of wood, rising up out of the forest and into the bright Texas sky.

TOWER HOUSE

© Art Gray

Il y a de petits cabanons des années 1930 situés le long du lac Travis, le plus long des *Highland Lakes*, qui parsèment la campagne jalonnée de collines à l'ouest d'Austin, et ils sont principalement utilisés en été. L'un d'eux se trouve sur un versant de coteau qui part du bord de l'eau pour monter sous une voûte d'espèces locales de chênes et de cèdres. Il comporte une grande pièce, une petite chambre à coucher, une cuisine, et un porche donnant sur le lac. Notre client voulait deux chambres supplémentaires avec leur salle-de-bain et un séjour pour réunir des groupes plus larges de personnes. Nous avons choisi de placer les nouveaux quartiers de nuit dans une tour séparée. Deux petites chambres occupent le premier et le second étage. Au-dessus, au troisième niveau, une terrasse s'ouvre sur un panorama du lac et des collines dans le lointain. Sur celle-ci, à quelques cent mètres au-dessus du sol, on peut profiter des après-midis les plus chauds de l'été sous un toit ouvert aux alizés dominants remontant du lac. Le cabanon en pierre d'origine est maintenant attenant à une tour verticale en bois, s'élevant de la forêt vers le ciel clair du Texas.

Esistono piccoli capanni in pietra calcarea risalenti agli anni '30, lungo il Lago Travis, il più lungo degli Highland Lakes, che si affacciano alla zona collinare a ovest di Austin, e che vengono utilizzati principalmente in estate. Uno di questi capanni si trova su un pendio che nasce dall'acqua, sotto un baldacchino di querce e cedri nativi. Era costituito da una grande stanza, una piccola camera da letto, una cucina e un portico prospiciente l'acqua. Il nostro cliente ha voluto aggiungervi due camere da letto con bagno e un'area living più capiente. Abbiamo scelto di organizzare la nuova zona notte in una torre separata. Il primo e il secondo piano sono occupati da due piccole camere da letto. Al terzo livello, una terrazza si apre al panorama sul lago e sulle dolci colline in lontananza. Su questa terrazza, a trenta metri circa di altezza, è possibile godersi persino il più caldo pomeriggio estivo, sotto una copertura aperta alle brezze rinfrescanti che soffiano dal lago. Il capanno in pietra originale si trova ora accanto alla torre verticale di legno, svettante al di sopra della foresta nel luminoso cielo del Texas.

Ground floor plan

Second floor plan

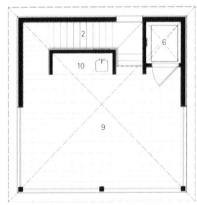

Third floor plan

1. Entry
2. Stair
3. Master bedroom
4. Bath
5. Machine room
6. Elevator
7. Landing
8. Bedroom
9. Roof terrace
10. Kitchenette

0   3m

The Bunny Run Boat Dock, located on the shore of Lake Austin, is an exploration of material and massing intended to look so blended into the site that it appears softly in a state of natural decomposition. The structure is an all exterior experience. Walls, ceilings and retractable screens create layers of enclosure. A variety of wood species –Sinker Cypress floors, articulated Cedar walls and a painted ceiling made of Douglas Fir–form an environment that is consistent with the natural wooded shoreline of the lake. The architectural palette is complemented by several reclaimed items: antique doors from India, a time worn butcher block from England and a steel structure that weathers naturally. The experience is intended to be an inviting homage to the beautiful climate and setting. A place to become connected to and surrounded by nature.

BUNNY RUN BOAT DOCK

© Andrew Pogue

Le Bunny Run Boat Dock, situé sur les rives du Lac Austin, est une exploration de matériaux et de volumes conçue pour se fondre dans le site au point d'avoir imperceptiblement l'air d'être en état de décomposition naturelle. Sa structure est une expérience complètement axée sur l'extérieur. Les murs, plafonds et panneaux escamotables créent des enveloppes d'enceinte. Une variété d'essences de bois, des sols en cyprès « trempé », des murs articulés en cèdre et un plafond peint construit en pin Douglas, forment un environnement qui est en cohérence avec le littoral boisé naturel du lac. Cette palette architecturale est complétée par plusieurs éléments recyclés : des portes anciennes provenant d'Inde, un bloc de boucher usé par le temps venant d'Angleterre et une structure métallique qui se corrode naturellement. Cette expérience se veut être un hommage accueillant à ce climat et ce cadre magnifiques. Un lieu auquel se connecter, entouré par la nature.

Il Bunny Run Boat Dock, ubicato sulle rive del Lago Austin, costituisce uno studio dei materiali e dei volumi realizzato per integrarsi nell'area al punto da apparire in uno stato di decomposizione naturale. La struttura è tutta all'aperto. Pareti, soffitti e schermi scorrevoli creano locali a strati. Una varietà di tipi di legno, pavimentazioni in cipresso, pareti articolate in cedro e un soffitto decorato in abete Douglas formano un ambiente che rispetta il litorale naturalmente boscoso del lago. La tavolozza architettonica è completata da numerosi elementi riciclati: le antiche porte dall'India, un consunto tavolo da macellaio dall'Inghilterra e una struttura in acciaio lasciata all'ossidazione naturale. L'esperienza vuole essere un invitante omaggio alla bellezza del clima e dello scenario. Un luogo dove lasciarsi circondare dalla natura, entrando in comunione con essa.

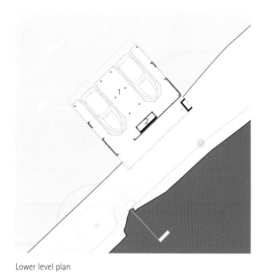

Lower level plan

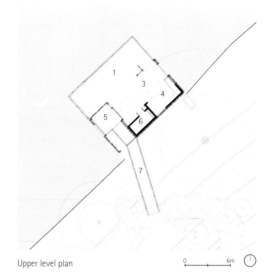

Upper level plan

1. Deck
2. Storage
3. Screened porch
4. Bar
5. Entry
6. Storage
7. Bridge

0   6m

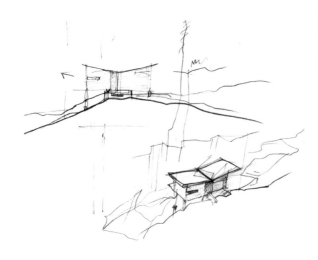

Locals call the granite and shale cliff overlooking Montana's Flathead Lake "The Matterhorn". It is a place to observe the natural world: the lake, the surrounding ponderosa pine forest, and especially the eagles and ospreys that nest nearby. Together, the water, cliff, and trees form a classic picture of the expansive American West, and it is clear why Montana is still known as North America's great destination. Within this context, the cabin's diaphanous volume is set on six steel piers that are delicately anchored to concrete blocks set into the slope. Screened walls enclose a living area, which has an open floor plan and wood slat floors that extend outside. Amenities are sparse but not neglected: a small kitchen, bathroom, and shower allow guests an overnight stay. The cabin has no heating or cooling system and running water is pumped from the lake below.

CABIN ON FLATHEAD LAKE

© Art Gray

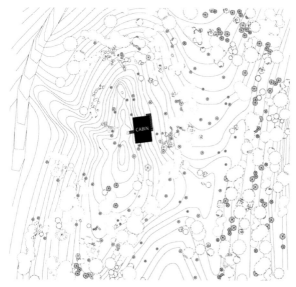

Site plan

Les habitants de la région appellent la falaise de granit et de schiste surplombant le lac Flathead du Montana le « Matterhorn ». C'est un endroit duquel on peut observer le monde naturel : le lac, la forêt de pins ponderosas, et surtout les aigles et balbuzards qui nichent dans les alentours. L'eau, la falaise, et les arbres forment ensemble une image iconique du vaste Ouest américain, et il n'est pas surprenant que le Montana soit toujours connu comme la destination majeure de l'Amérique du Nord. Dans ce contexte, le volume diaphane du cabanon est fixé sur six pilotis d'acier qui sont délicatement scellés à des blocs de béton ancrés dans la pente. Des murs écrans entourent un espace à vivre, en plan ouvert, dont les sols en lattes de bois se prolongent à l'extérieur. Les commodités sont limitées sans être négligées : une petite cuisine, une salle-de-bain, et une douche permettent à des invités de passer la nuit. Ce cabanon ne dispose ni de chauffage ni de climatisation et l'eau courante est pompée du lac en contrebas.

La gente del luogo chiama la parete rocciosa di granito e scisto che guarda sul Lago Flathead del Montana "The Matterhorn". È il posto ideale per osservare il regno della Natura: il lago, la foresta di pini gialli tutta intorno, e soprattutto le aquile e i falchi pescatori che nidificano lì vicino. Insieme, l'acqua, la roccia e gli alberi formano la classica immagine del vasto Ovest americano, e non stupisce che il Montana sia ancora oggi considerato come la grande destinazione del Nord America. In questo contesto, il volume diafano del capanno si erge da sei pilastri in acciaio ancorati a blocchi di calcestruzzo, a loro volta fissati al pendio. Muri schermati racchiudono l'area living, con una pianta aperta e la pavimentazione in assi di legno che si estendono fino all'aperto. Le comodità sono rade, ma non trascurate: una piccola cucina, un bagno e la doccia consentono agli ospiti di pernottare nella struttura. Il capanno non è dotato di riscaldamento o climatizzazione, e l'acqua viene pompata direttamente dal lago sottostante.

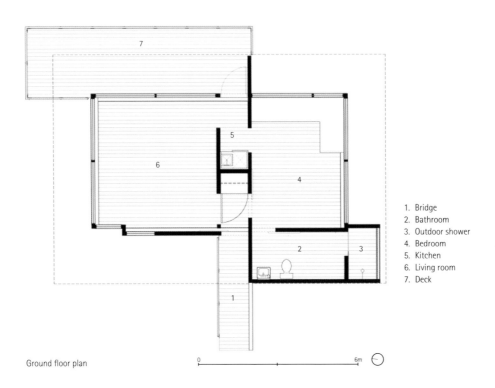

Ground floor plan

0   6m

1. Bridge
2. Bathroom
3. Outdoor shower
4. Bedroom
5. Kitchen
6. Living room
7. Deck

atelierjones' work entwines design and research to embrace methodologies mined from sustainability and materials research, high-performance building systems from mass timber to modular prefabrication, historic preservation and adaptive reuse strategies and real estate development as well as community activism. We build homes, infill urban housing, shops, churches, offices, schools, gardens, theaters, prayer chapels and biodiesel stations. Founded by Susan Jones, FAIA in 2003 the firm seeks out sites, buildings and materials with inherent, but underutilized value —to harvest their embodied energy, their catalytic power for owners and communities to create new, innovative and beautiful design. atelierjones' award-winning work is founded on research, teaching and community engagement to envision new systemic, cross-disciplinary sustainable strategies for buildings, including innovative work with mass timber; we recently completed four of the first mass timber strucutures built in the US.

ATELIERJONES

WWW.ATELIERJONES.COM

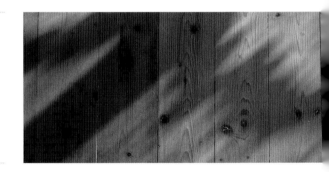

Le travail d'atelierjones mêle le design et la recherche pour mettre en application des méthodologies tirées de la recherche sur la durabilité et les matériaux, les systèmes de construction haute performance du bois massif à la préfabrication modulaire, de la conservation historique et des stratégies de réutilisation adaptive au développement immobilier et à l'activisme communautaire. Nous construisons des maisons, des « dents creuses » de l'habitat urbain, des magasins, des églises, des écoles, des jardins, des théâtres, des chapelles de prière et des stations de biodiesel. Fondé par Susan Jones, FAIA, en 2003, ce cabinet cherche des sites, des bâtiments et des matériaux ayant une valeur intrinsèque, mais sous-utilisée – pour recueillir leur énergie grise, leur puissance catalytique pour que les propriétaires et les communautés créent de nouveau designs, beaux et novateurs. Les travaux primés d'atelierjones sont fondés sur la recherche, l'enseignement et l'engagement communautaire pour imaginer de nouvelles stratégies systémiques, interdisciplinaires pour les constructions, y compris un travail innovant avec du bois massif.

Il lavoro dello studio atelierjones intreccia progettazione e ricerca per abbracciare le metodologie derivanti dagli studi sulla sostenibilità e i materiali, i sistemi edilizi ad alta prestazione dal mass timber ai prefabbricati modulari, le strategie di conservazione storica e riuso adattivo, la costruzione di immobili e l'attivismo comunitario. Costruiamo case, completiamo edilizia abitativa urbana, negozi, chiese, uffici, scuole, giardini, teatri, luoghi di preghiera e stazioni di biocarburante. Fondato da Susan Jones, FAIA nel 2003, lo studio individua siti, costruzioni e materiali con un valore intrinseco ma sottostimato, per coglierne l'energia, il potere catalizzatore per i proprietari e le comunità, e creare progetti nuovi e innovativi di grande bellezza. Il lavoro pluripremiato di atelierjones si basa sulla ricerca, sull'insegnamento e sul coinvolgimento della comunità nell'immaginare nuove strategie sostenibili, sistemiche e interdisciplinari per l'edilizia, incluse le nuove opere con mass timber.

CLT HOUSE
CLT CHURCH

Site plan

The CLT House is a modest, 1,500 sf single-family house for four in Seattle. The project was driven by the different parameters of a small, triangular lot, the need for a light-filled, Urban Cabin and the desire for heritage Pacific Northwest materials. Cross-laminated timber (CLT), commonplace in Europe, emerging building material in the US, was a natural choice to fulfill these requirements. The house experiments with this new tectonic; it is the first in Seattle and one of the first structures in the US to use CLT. The structural use of CLT, rawly revealed on the interior, creates a visceral, natural, yet constructed experience: the hypernatural; the CLT is employed as structure and has a high carbon sequestration capacity. Achieving a Built Green 5-star rating, using PassivHaus detailing, targeting 38% lower energy use than Washington State Energy Code, CLT House was a research vehicle for the firm and is being openly shared with a broad interdisciplinary CLT community across the US.

CLT HOUSE

© Lara Swimmer

La CLT House est une modeste maison de presque 140 mètres carrés conçue pour une famille de quatre à Seattle. Ce projet a été amené par les différents paramètres d'une parcelle petite et triangulaire, la nécessité de créer un cabanon urbain rempli de lumière et le désir d'utiliser des matériaux traditionnels du Nord-ouest du Pacifique. Le bois stratifié croisé, CLT, commun en Europe, émergeant en tant que matériau de construction aux États-Unis, était un choix naturel pour remplir ces conditions. Cette maison expérimente cette nouvelle tectonique ; c'est la première de Seattle et l'une des premières structures aux États-Unis à utiliser le CLT. Cette utilisation structurelle du CLT, révélée de façon brute à l'intérieur, crée une expérience viscérale, naturelle, mais construite : l'hypernaturel ; le CLT est employé comme structure et a une haute capacité de séquestration du carbone. Avec une classification 5 étoiles dans le bâti écologique, en utilisant les spécifications PassivHaus, visant une économie d'énergie 38% plus basse que le Code énergétique de l'Etat de Washington, la CLT House a été un véhicule de recherche pour le cabinet et fait l'objet de partages avec une large communauté CLT interdisciplinaire dans tous les États-Unis.

CLT House è una modesta dimora da 140 metri quadrati per una famiglia di quattro componenti, sita in Seattle. Il progetto si è evoluto secondo le diverse esigenze dettate da un lotto piccolo a pianta triangolare, dalla richiesta di un cottage urbano pieno di luce e dal desiderio di materiali della tradizione del Nord-Ovest del Pacifico. Il legno lamellare a strati incrociati (CLT), materiale comune in Europa ma ancora emergente negli Stati Uniti, è stata la scelta naturale per soddisfare tutti i requisiti. La casa è la prima a Seattle in questo nuovo materiale, e una delle prime in assoluto negli USA. L'uso strutturale del CLT, che si rivela negli interni rustici, genera un'esperienza viscerale, naturale, eppure solida: quella dell'iper-naturale. Il CLT viene impiegato come struttura e ha un'elevata capacità di sequestro del carbonio. Con la sua valutazione Built Green a 5 stelle, i dettagli PassivHaus, l'utilizzo di energia minore del 38% rispetto al Washington State Energy Code, CLT House si è rivelata veicolo di ricerca per lo studio, e sta sperimentando una condivisione che coinvolge l'ampia comunità interdisciplinare interessata al CLT in tutti gli USA.

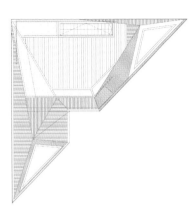

Roof plan

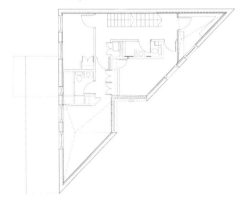

Second floor plan

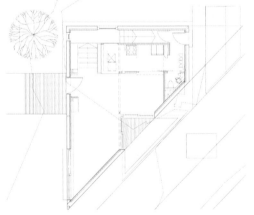

Ground floor plan

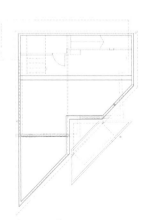

Basement plan

North elevation

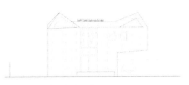

South elevation

East elevation

West elevation

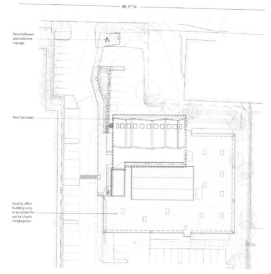

Site plan

0 5m

One of the oldest churches in the exurban tech city outside of Seattle, the First Congregational Church congregation was established in 1896. In 2013, the church adapted a classic low-rise suburban 1970's office building into their future space of worship and community outreach. Within the strict grid of the two-story building, the new form of the sanctuary pushes out existing walls and roof, creating a new definitive form within the existing matrix. Delineation between the northern interior wall and ceiling was collapsed by using Cross-Laminated-Timber (CLT) panels; the CLT panels are inserted as an irregular, folded plate structure insuring both greater structural stability as well as a rich interplay of light, shadow and the warm texture of the Canadian White Pine of the white-washed CLT panels. Use of CLT highlights the Pacific Northwest's regional relationship to timber, reduces the project's overall carbon footprint, and humanizes the cold sterility of the existing building.

CLT CHURCH

© Lara Swimmer

L'une des plus vieilles églises de la « tech city » exurbaine des faubourgs de Seattle, la congrégation de la *First Congregational Church* a été établie en 1896. En 2013, cette église a adapté un bâtiment classique des banlieues des années 1970 de faible hauteur pour en faire leur futur espace de culte et de communication avec le public. Dans les limites de la grille stricte de l'immeuble de deux étages, la nouvelle forme de ce sanctuaire pousse les murs et le toit existants, créant une nouvelle forme définitive au sein de la matrice d'origine. La délimitation entre l'intérieur du mur nord et du plafond a été abaissée à l'aide de panneaux de CLT ; les panneaux sont insérés en une structure plissée irrégulière garantissant à la fois une plus grande stabilité et un splendide jeu de lumières et d'ombres ainsi que la chaleureuse texture du pin blanc canadien des panneaux de CLT patinés. L'usage du CLT souligne la relation du nord-ouest pacifique avec le bois, réduit l'empreinte carbone globale du projet, et humanise la froide stérilité du bâtiment d'origine.

Una delle più antiche chiese della tech city extraurbana di Seattle, la prima chiesa congregazionale fondata nel 1896. Nel 2013, la chieda ha adattato un classico edificio di uffici suburbano e basso, risalente agli anni '70 come futuro spazio di preghiera e sensibilizzazione della comunità. All'interno della rigida griglia della costruzione a due piani, la nuova forma del luogo sacro spinge verso l'esterno pareti e tetto, creando una nuova forma definitiva dalla matrice esistente. La limitazione tra la parete interna a nord e il soffitto è stata abbattuta tramite l'uso di pannelli in legno lamellare a strati incrociati (CLT); i pannelli in CLT si inseriscono come struttura irregolare a piastra piegata, garantendo una maggiore stabilità strutturale e una ricca interazione tra luce e ombra. Il calore del pino bianco canadese è dato dal bianco dei pannelli in CLT. L'uso del CLT mette in evidenza il rapporto della regione del Nord-Ovest Pacifico con il legname, riduce l'impronta di carbonio complessiva del progetto e umanizza la fredda sterilità dell'edificio preesistente.

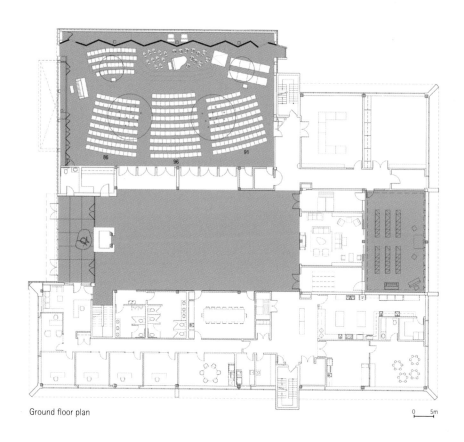

Ground floor plan

0   5m

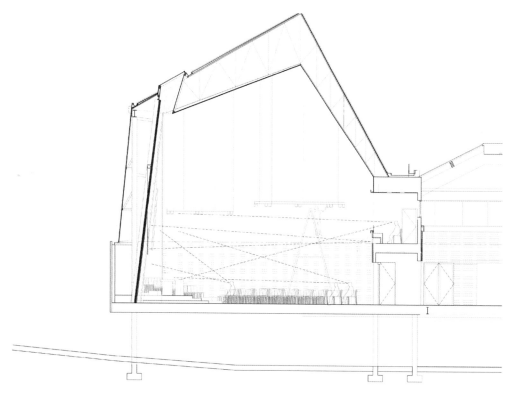

Section

——— Cross laminated timber wall

Atelier Oslo is an architectural office established in 2006. Founded by Nils Ole Bae Brandtzæg, Thomas Liu, Marius Mowe and Jonas Norsted. Atelier Oslo's portfolio includes projects ranging from large cultural projects to single family houses and small installations. The development of each project focus on creating architecture of high quality in which the basic elements of architecture such as structure, materiality, light and space are particularly emphasized and reinterpreted in order to solve current challenges. Atelier Oslo has won numerous architectural competitions, including the international competition for the new central library of Oslo, Deichman, in collaboration with Lund Hagem.

ATELIER OSLO

WWW.ATELIEROSLO.NO

Atelier Oslo est un cabinet d'architecture fondé en 2006 par Nils Ole Bae Brandtzæg, Thomas Liu, Marius Mowe et Jonas Norsted. Son portefeuille comporte des projets allant des plus grandes programmations culturelles à des maisons unifamiliales et de petites installations. Le développement de chaque projet se concentre sur la création d'une architecture de grande qualité dans laquelle les éléments de base de l'architecture tels que la structure, la matérialité, la lumière et l'espace sont particulièrement mis en valeur et réinterprétés afin de résoudre les défis actuels. Atelier Oslo a remporté de nombreux prix d'architecture, y compris la compétition internationale pour la nouvelle bibliothèque d'Oslo, Deichman, en collaboration avec Lund Hagem.

Atelier Oslo è uno studio di architettura che opera dal 2006. I suoi fondatori sono Nils Ole Bae Brandtzæg, Thomas Liu, Marius Mowe e Jonas Norsted. I lavori di Atelier Oslo includono progetti che spaziano dai grandi edifici dati alla cultura, alle case unifamiliari, fino alle piccole installazioni. Lo sviluppo di ciascun progetto si concentra sul creare un'architettura di alta qualità, nell'ambito della quale gli elementi di base come struttura, materialità, luce e spazio siano valorizzati in modo particolare e reinterpretati per risolvere le sfide di oggi. Atelier Oslo ha vinto numerosi concorsi di architettura, incluso quello internazionale per la nuova biblioteca centrale di Oslo, Deichman, in collaborazione con Lund Hagem.

VILLA HOLTET

HOUSE ON AN ISLAND

CABIN NORDERHOV

The starting point for this task was a typical challenge in Oslo: densification in an area of existing single family houses. The plot was a lovely old garden. It was important for us to preserve much of the garden, therefore, the ground floor has a relatively limited footprint, while the larger upper floor cantilevers out creating covered outdoor areas. The house is broken up into smaller volumes to adapt to the relatively tight situation and the scale of the surrounding buildings. As an addition to the garden, and as compensation for the reduced view, the project creates an inner landscape, a sequence of rooms with varying scale and use, different degrees of transparency and privacy, changing views and light conditions. The central double height living room is the heart of the house and connects all the rooms and areas. The room is surrounded in first floor by lobby, kitchen and dining room, and the garden with its various outdoor areas. A staircase leads up to a gallery with access to bedrooms and bathrooms. A large skylight provides varied light and shadow effects through the day. The house structure is prefabricated wooden columns and beams. All structure parts are exposed in the interior of the project.

Site plan

VILLA HOLTET

© Lars Petter Pettersen, Gunnar Sørås

Le point de départ de cette mission était un challenge typique d'Oslo : la densification dans une zone de maisons unifamiliales existantes. La parcelle était un ancien jardin ravissant. Comme il était important pour nous de conserver une partie importante de ce jardin, le rez-de-chaussée a une empreinte relativement réduite, tandis que l'étage supérieur, plus étendu, déborde en porte-à-faux en créant des zones extérieures couvertes. La maison est découpée en plus petits volumes pour l'adapter à sa situation relativement étroite et à l'échelle des immeubles environnants. Pour compenser la vue réduite, ce projet crée un paysage intérieur, une séquence de pièces à échelles et usages variés, aux différents degrés de transparence et d'intimité, aux vues et aux conditions d'éclairage changeantes. Le séjour central en double hauteur représente le cœur de la maison et relie toutes les pièces et les zones entre elles. Cette pièce est entourée au premier étage par le lobby, la cuisine et la salle-à-manger, et le jardin avec ses zones extérieures diverses. Un escalier mène à une galerie avec accès aux chambres et aux salles-de-bain. Une grande fenêtre de toit apporte une variété d'effets de lumière et d'ombres tout au long de la journée. La structure de la maison est faite de colonnes et de poutres préfabriquées.

Il punto di partenza di questo incarico rappresentava una sfida tipica, per Oslo: ridensificare un'area residenziale di piccole case unifamiliari. Il lotto era costituito da un bellissimo giardino antico. Per noi era importante preservare gran parte del giardino. Abbiamo quindi optato per un piano terra dalla pianta relativamente limitata, e realizzare un livello superiore più ampio, che sporge creando aree esterne coperte. La casa è suddivisa in volumi più piccoli, per adattarsi alla situazione relativamente ristretta e alle dimensioni degli edifici circostanti. In aggiunta al giardino e per compensare la scarsa apertura panoramica, il progetto ha realizzato un paesaggio interno: una sequenza di stanze con dimensioni e usi variabili, diversi gradi di trasparenza e privacy, condizioni di luce e di vista cangianti. La zona living centrale a doppia altezza è il cuore della casa e collega tutte le stanze e le aree. La stanza è circondata al primo piano dall'ingresso, la cucina e la zona pranzo, oltre che dal giardino, con i suoi diversi spazi esterni. Una scala porta fino a una galleria con accesso alle camere da letto e ai bagni. Un grande lucernario genera effetti diversi di luce e ombra nel corso della giornata. La struttura della casa è costituita da travi e colonne in legno prefabbricate.

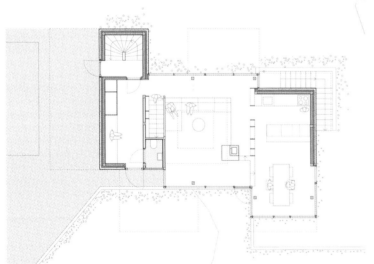

Ground floor plan

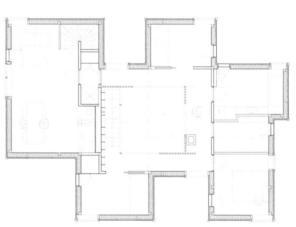

First floor plan

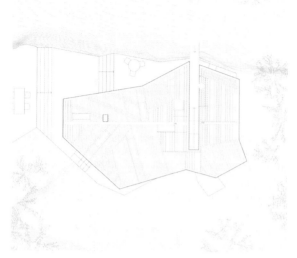

Site plan

The small house is situated on an island on the south coast of Norway. The site is characterized by smooth and curved rocks that goes down towards the ocean. The topography of the site was carefully measured to integrate the rocks into the project. Concrete floors in different levels connect to the main levels of the topography and create a variety of different outdoor spaces. The concrete floors and stairs dissolve the division of inside and outside. The interior becomes part of the landscape and walking in and around the cabin gives a unique experience, where the different qualities from the site becomes part of the architecture. A prefabricated timber structure is placed on the concrete floors and at last a light wood structure covers the cabin to filter the light and direct the views. The wood structure has a depth that creates a play of shadows through the day and a calm atmosphere resembling the feeling of sitting under a tree. A small annex creates a fence towards the neighbor building and another sheltered outdoor space. All exterior wood is Kebony which is a special heat- treated wood that will turn grey and require no maintenance.

HOUSE ON AN ISLAND

© Nils Vik, Thomas Liu, Charlotte Thiis-Evensen

La petite maison est située sur une île sur la côte sud de la Norvège. Ce site est caractérisé par des rochers lisses et arrondis qui descendent vers l'Océan. La topographie de ce site a été soigneusement mesurée pour intégrer les rochers au projet. Des sols en béton à différents niveaux font le lien avec les niveaux principaux de la topographie et créent une variété d'espaces extérieurs différents. Les sols et les marches en béton dissipent la rupture entre l'intérieur et l'extérieur. L'intérieur s'intègre dans le paysage et se promener dans et autour de la cabine offre une expérience unique, dans laquelle les différentes qualités du site deviennent des parties intégrantes de l'architecture. Une structure en bois préfabriquée est placée sur des sols en béton et une structure légère en bois recouvre l'habitation pour filtrer la lumière et orienter les vues. La structure en bois est dotée d'une profondeur qui crée un jeu d'ombres au cours de la journée et une atmosphère calme évoquant la sensation d'être assis sous un arbre. Une petite annexe crée une barrière vers la maison du voisin et un autre espace extérieur abrité. Tout le bois extérieur est en Kebony, bois norvégien qui, thermo-traité, deviendra gris et ne nécessitera aucun entretien.

La piccola casa si trova in Norvegia, su un'isola della costa meridionale. L'area è caratterizzata da rocce lisce e curve, che si allungano verso l'oceano. La topografia del sito è stata misurata con cura, per poter integrare le rocce nel progetto. I pavimenti di calcestruzzo a diversi livelli si rifanno ai livelli della topografia e creano una varietà di spazi esterni diversi tra loro. I pavimenti e le scale in calcestruzzo dissolvono la separazione tra interno ed esterno. L'interno diviene parte del paesaggio e camminare dentro e intorno alla baita regala un'esperienza unica, in cui le diverse qualità dell'area diventano parte dell'architettura. Sui pavimenti di calcestruzzo è posta una struttura prefabbricata in legno, e infine il rivestimento leggero di legno che copre tutta la baita filtra la luce e orienta i panorami. La struttura in legno ha una profondità che crea un gioco di ombre durante il giorno, e un'atmosfera tranquilla che richiama la sensazione di sedere sotto un albero. Una piccola dependance separa il complesso dalla costruzione adiacente, creando un altro spazio esterno riparato. Tutto il legno per esterni è in Kebony, uno speciale legname trattato termicamente, che diviene grigio e non richiede manutenzione.

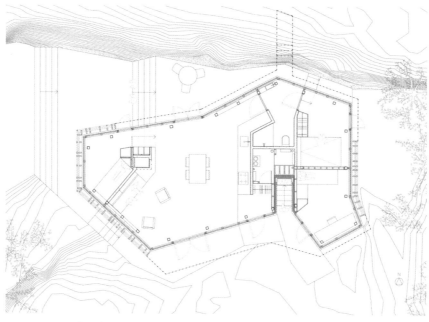

Floor plan

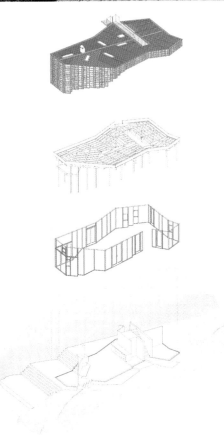

Axonometric view

The project is located in Krokskogen forests. Its location on a steep slope gives a fantastic view over the lake Steinsfjorden. The site is often exposed to strong winds, so the cabin is organized around several outdoors spaces that provide shelter from the wind and receives the sun at different times of the day. The interior is a shaped as a continuous space. The curved walls and ceilings form continuous surfaces clad with birch plywood. The floor follows the terrain and divides the plan into several levels that also defines the different functional zones of the cabin. Large glass walls are located in the living and dining areas. This creates a more direct relationship with the nature outside. Outside, the cottage has a more rectangular geometry and the walls and roofs are covered with basalt stone slabs laid in a pattern similar the ones often used for traditional wooden claddings in Norway. The lodge consists mainly of prefabricated elements. The main structure is laminated timber completed with a substructure of *Kerto* construction plywood. The cabin is supported by steel rods drilled directly into the rock, supplemented with a small concrete foundation under the fireplace for stabilization.

CABIN NORDERHOV

© Lars Petter Pettersen, Atelier Oslo

Ce projet est situé dans les forêts de Krokskogen. Son emplacement sur une colline pentue offre une vue fantastique sur le lac Steinsfjorden. Ce site est souvent exposé à des vents violents, de sorte que le cabanon est organisé autour de plus espaces extérieurs qui protègent du vent et il reçoit le soleil à différents moments de la journée. L'intérieur est un espace continu. Les murs et plafonds cintrés forment des surfaces continues bardées de contreplaqué de bouleau. Le sol suit le terrain et divise le plan en plusieurs niveaux qui définissent également les différentes zones fonctionnelles du cabanon. De grandes cloisons vitrées sont situées dans les coin-séjour et coin-repas. Cela crée une relation plus directe avec la nature. À l'extérieur, le cottage est plus rectangulaire et ses murs et toitures sont recouverts de dalles de basalte posées d'une façon similaire à celles qui étaient souvent utilisées pour les habillages en lattes de bois traditionnels en Norvège. Le pavillon est majoritairement composé d'éléments préfabriqués. La structure principale est en bois laminé complété d'une substructure de contreplaqué de construction *Kerto*. Le cabanon est soutenu par des tiges d'acier directement vissées dans la roche, complétées par une petite fondation en béton sous la cheminée pour stabiliser l'ensemble.

Il progetto si trova nelle foreste di Krokskogen. La posizione in pendenza apre la vista sul magnifico lago Steinsfjorden. L'area è spesso battuta da forti venti; per questo, la baita è sviluppata intorno a molti spazi esterni che offrono riparo dalle correnti e ricevono la luce del sole a diverse ore del giorno. L'interno è realizzato come uno spazio senza interruzioni. I muri e i soffitti ricurvi formano superfici continue, rivestite con multistrato di betulla. Il pavimento si svolge seguendo la morfologia del suolo e suddivide il piano in livelli diversi che definiscono anche le diverse funzioni dello spazio interno. Le zone living e da pranzo hanno ampie pareti vetrate. Ciò crea un rapporto più diretto con la natura. Fuori, il cottage ha una geometria più rettangolare, e i muri e i tetti sono rivestiti con lastre di roccia di basalto posate in modo simile ai rivestimenti in legno tipici della Norvegia. La costruzione si compone per lo più di elementi prefabbricati. La struttura principale è in legno lamellare, completata da una sottostruttura in multistrato *Kerto*. La baita si sostiene su barre in acciaio inserite direttamente nella roccia, integrate da una piccola fondamenta in calcestruzzo, posta sotto il camino come elemento stabilizzante.

Floor plan

Alexandra Barker is the Assistant Chair of the Graduate Architecture and Urban Design Department in the School of Architecture at Pratt Institute, an associate professor with CCE (Certificate of Continuing Education), and the coordinator of the Masters in Architecture program. She has previously taught in the graduate architecture department at the University of Pennsylvania and in the undergraduate architecture department at Princeton University. At Pratt, she has been the recipient of national grants to integrate practice and education and sustainable principles into Pratt's graduate architecture curriculum.

Alexandra Barker received her MArch from Harvard University's Graduate School of Design, where she received the Templeton Kelly Prize and the Clifford Wong Housing Prize for her thesis work. Her undergraduate work in Visual and Environmental Studies was completed at Harvard College, where she graduated magna cum laude.

BFDO
ARCHITECTS

WWW.BARKERFREEMAN.COM

Alexandra Barker est vice-présidente du département d'architecture et de design urbain de l'École d'architecture de l'Institut Pratt, *Associate professor* titulaire d'un CCE (*Certificate of Continuing Education*), et coordinatrice du programme de Mastère en Architecture. Elle a enseigné dans le département d'architecture de l'Université de Pennsylvanie et celui de l'Université de Princeton. A Pratt, elle a reçu des subventions nationales pour intégrer pratique, éducation et principes durables dans le programme d'architecture de cet Institut.

Alexandra Barker a reçu son MArch de la *Graduate School of Design* de l'Université d'Harvard, où le *Templeton Kelly Prize* et le *Clifford Wong Housing Prize* lui ont été attribués pour ses travaux de thèse. Elle a achevé ses études de premier cycle à Harvard où elle a obtenu son diplôme avec mention (*magna cum laude*).

Alexandra Barker è l'Assistente alla Cattedra del Dipartimento di Architettura e Design Urbano del Pratt Institute, docente associato con CCE (Certificate of Continuing Education), e coordinatrice del programma Master in Architettura. In precedenza, ha insegnato nel dipartimento di architettura dell'Università della Pennsylvania e nel corso pre-laurea di architettura dell'Università di Princeton. Al Pratt ha ricevuto sovvenzioni nazionali per integrare la pratica e l'istruzione dei principi di sostenibilità nel corso di studi di architettura.

Alexandra Barker ha ricevuto il MArch dalla Scuola di Design di Harvard, dove ha ricevuto anche il Templeton Kelly Prize e il Clifford Wong Housing Prize per il suo lavoro di tesi. Ha completato il corso pre-laurea sugli Studi Visivi e Ambientali presso Harvard, dove si è laureata con lode.

20TH STREET TOWNHOUSE   SURFBOARD HOUSE   DEEP POINT HOUSE

For this renovation, the existing building volume was carved and expanded to carefully proportion room sizes, sequences, and adjacencies, and to capture daylight with generously-sized skylights, window walls and glazed corners. Rectangles of gray-stained tongue and groove Atlantic white cedar siding wrap the entries and slide around corners to emphasize the volumetric shifts in the façade. A covered porch with a wraparound corner window is carved from the front extension. A large skylight above the relocated stairwell brings more daylight to the first floor. The widened rear extension creates a generous mahogany-paneled kitchen and office nook. A deck off the kitchen extends the materiality of the interior living space out into the yard. Upstairs, corner-wrapping windows take advantage of the open skies to bring generous amounts of light into the kids' bedrooms. Cement tile and ceramic mosaics in graphic patterns of blue and white enliven the bathrooms.

20TH STREET TOWNHOUSE

© Francis Dzikowski

Pour cette rénovation, le volume d'origine du bâtiment a été découpé et augmenté pour proportionner judicieusement les pièces, séquences et contiguïtés, et pour capter la lumière du jour par le biais de fenêtres de toit aux proportions généreuses, de cloisons et d'angles vitrés. Des rectangles de parement composés d'un assemblage de rainures et languettes en cèdre blanc de l'Atlantique teint en gris entourent l'entrée et courent le long des angles pour accentuer les effets volumétriques de la façade. Un porche couvert doté d'une fenêtre d'angle panoramique est découpé dans l'extension de façade. Une large fenêtre de toit au-dessus du nouvel escalier apporte un surcroît de lumière au premier étage. L'extension arrière élargie crée une cuisine lambrissée d'acajou et un coin bureau. Un deck adjacent à la cuisine prolonge la matérialité de l'espace de vie intérieur jusque dans la cour. À l'étage, des fenêtres panoramiques d'angle tirent parti du ciel dégagé pour apporter une abondance de lumière dans les chambres des enfants. Des dalles de ciment et des mosaïques de céramique égayent les salles-de-bain avec des motifs graphiques bleu et blanc.

Per questa ristrutturazione, il volume dell'edificio preesistente è stato plasmato ed esteso per dare la giusta proporzione alle camere, alla sequenza degli spazi e alle adiacenze, e catturare la luce naturale attraverso ampi lucernari, pareti finestrate e vetrate ad angolo. Inserti in grigio si incastrano nel tono naturale del cedro dell'Atlante, incorniciando gli ingressi e scivolando lungo gli angoli per esaltare le variazioni volume-triche della facciata. Dall'estensione frontale è stato ricavato un portico coperto con un'avvolgente finestra ad angolo. L'ampio lucernario sulla scalinata ricollocata favorisce l'illuminazione naturale del primo piano. L'estensione posteriore ampliata crea una spaziosa cucina rivestita in mogano e l'angolo ufficio. Il ballatoio esterno alla cucina espande la materialità dello spazio interno fino alla corte esterna. Al piano di sopra, le fi-nestre ad angolo sfruttano al meglio i cieli aperti e inondano di luce le camere da letto dei bambini. Piastrelle in cemento e mosaici in ceramica dai motivi bianchi e blu ravvivano i bagni.

Second floor plan

Ground floor plan

Basement plan

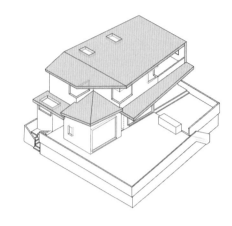

Five years after Hurricane Sandy wreaked havoc on the coastline of New York City, the Surfboard House was completed. The waterfront lot was the site of a house washed away by the storm, and stricter flood regulations resulted in a shallow building volume sited lengthwise along the oceanfront. The beachfront facade steps to allow windows to wrap corners and creates diagonal sightlines up and down the beach. A raised cedar-clad ceiling defines the living room, with nine-foot tall sliding glass doors and a diagonally pitched roof. Beyond the kitchen, the first floor master bedroom has wraparound windows looking east toward undeveloped beach frontage and opens out to a deck that steps down for privacy. Upstairs, compact bedrooms feel expansive thanks to corner views, and a media room opens onto a covered deck. White cedar cladding wraps the building and roof overhangs. The fiberglass-wrapped roof culminates in a large 'surfboard' overhang that protects the first floor from solar heat gain.

SURFBOARD HOUSE

© Francis Dzikowski

Cinq ans après les dévastations occasionnées par l'ouragan Sandy sur la côte de New York City, la Surfboard House a été terminée. Cette parcelle au bord de l'eau était le site d'une maison emportée par la tempête, et la réglementation plus stricte en matière d'inondations a entraîné la construction d'un volume peu profond positionné dans le sens de la longueur, en suivant le bord de l'océan. La façade côté plage est échelonnée pour permettre aux fenêtres de couvrir les angles et crée des perspectives diagonales de part et d'autre de la plage. Un plafond surélevé bardé de cèdre définit le séjour, avec ses portes vitrées coulissantes de 2,7 m et son toit en diagonale. Derrière la cuisine, la suite principale est dotée de fenêtres panoramiques donnant à l'est sur une partie de plage inexploitée et ouvre sur une terrasse en contrebas pour plus d'intimité. À l'étage, des chambres compactes paraissent spacieuses grâce à des vues d'angle, et une salle multimédia donne sur un deck couvert. Un bardage de cèdre blanc enveloppe le bâtiment et les avant-toits. La toiture recouverte de fibre de verre culmine en une « planche de surf » en porte-à-faux qui protège le premier étage de la chaleur solaire.

Cinque anni dopo l'azione devastante dell'Uragano Sandy sulle coste di New York City, Surfboard House è stata completata. La zona litoranea ospitava una casa spazzata via dalla tempesta, e le severe norme di protezione dalle inondazioni hanno dato come risultato una costruzione bassa, ubicata di fronte all'oceano. La facciata sul mare avanza per consentire alle finestre di avvolgere gli angoli e crea visuali diagonali della spiaggia. La zona soggiorno è definita da un soffitto rivestito in cedro, con porte a vetri scorrevoli alte quasi tre metri e un tetto spiovente. Oltre la cucina, la camera da letto padronale al primo piano ha finestre avvolgenti che guardano a est verso una spiaggia incontaminata e si apre su un ballatoio che scorre verso il basso per garantire la privacy. Al piano di sopra, le camere da letto più ridotte acquistano ampiezza grazie alle visuali angolate, e una sala multimediale si apre sul ballatoio coperto. L'intera costruzione e le sporgenze del tetto sono rivestite di cedro bianco. Il tetto ricoperto di fibra di vetro culmina in un'ampia sporgenza a 'tavola da surf' che protegge il primo piano dall'eccessiva luce solare.

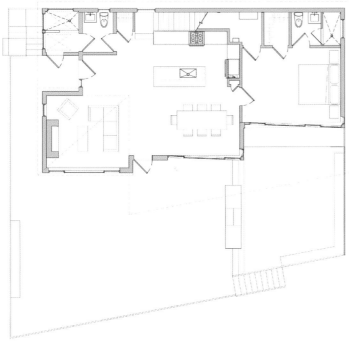

Ground floor plan

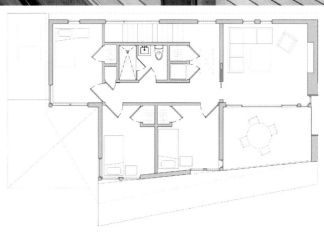

Second floor plan

A 1950s ranch house was taken down to its foundation to enlarge the house and to make the most of its 17-acre site overlooking two converging creeks. A new entry on the east facade divides the original south-facing volume from the den extension to the north, creating a breezeway with a water view and access to a wraparound deck. An exterior stair continues the breezeway sequence, which culminates in a rooftop garden. Inside, the living spaces feature a three-sided, storefront-like glass enclosure offering views to the south, west and north, with large sliding doors leading to the deck. The open plan of the kitchen, living and dining rooms is punctuated by a two-sided fireplace, which separates dining and living areas. Skylights on either side allow light to bounce off the surface of the chimney volume. Outside, planted rows of herbs and flowers comprise a "capsule farm" on the rooftop and the flora delineates an outdoor seating area.

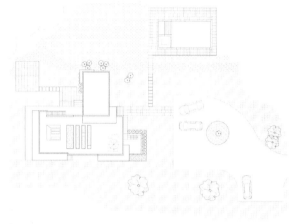

Site plan

DEEP POINT HOUSE

© Francis Dzikowski

Cette habitation de 1950 située sur un ranch a été réduite à ses fondations pour l'élargir et profiter du site de presque 7 hectares donnant sur la confluence de deux ruisseaux. Une nouvelle entrée sur la façade est divise le volume originel orienté sud de l'extension de salle commune vers le nord, créant un passage couvert avec une vue sur l'eau et un accès au deck de pourtour. Un escalier extérieur continue la séquence de ce passage, qui culmine en un jardin terrasse. À l'intérieur, les espaces à vivre comportent une enceinte vitrée à trois pans, rappelant une devanture de magasin, avec des vues en direction du sud, de l'ouest, et du nord, et de grandes portes coulissantes menant à la terrasse. Le plan ouvert de la cuisine, du séjour et de la salle-à-manger est rythmé par un foyer à deux faces qui sépare le coin repas et le coin séjour. Les fenêtres de toit de chaque côté font ricocher la lumière sur la surface du volume de l'âtre. À l'extérieur, des rangées d'herbes aromatiques et de fleurs forment une « ferme miniature » sur le toit et la flore délimite une zone banquette extérieure.

Un casale degli anni '50 è stato abbattuto fino alle fondamenta per ampliarne la pianta e trarre il massimo dai 7 ettari circa, affacciati su due insenature convergenti. Un nuovo ingresso sulla facciata est divide il volume originale rivolto a sud dall'estensione del salotto verso nord, creando un corridoio coperto con panorama sull'acqua e accesso a un ballatoio che circonda l'intera costruzione. Una scala esterna continua lo scorrere del corridoio coperto, culminando nel giardino sul tetto. All'interno, gli spazi abitativi sono caratterizzati da una vetrata a tre lati, che mima la vetrina di un negozio e apre i panorami sui lati sud, ovest e nord, con ampie porte scorrevoli che danno sul ballatoio. L'open space che include cucina, soggiorno e sala da pranzo è esaltato da un caminetto a due facce che separa la zona pranzo da quella del soggiorno. I lucernari su entrambi i lati creano giochi di luce sulle pareti del caminetto. All'esterno, file di erbe e fiori compongono una "capsule farm", una fattoria in miniatura, sul tetto, e la flora delinea l'area relax.

Birdseye is a renowned design studio in Richmond, Vermont, practicing architecture and interior design services for private clients. Founded in 1997 by principal architect Brian J. Mac, FAIA, the firm specializes in bespoke residential design. Seen throughout northeastern America, the work reflects a continued evaluation and refinement of art + craft, firmly rooted in the building tradition of place. Design concepts are derived through a thoughtful, iterative exploration of both the literal and the abstract. Birdseye is the recipient of several international design awards and numerous American Institute of Architects honors, both locally and regionally. The firm is a participant in the 2018 Time Space Existence architectural exhibition, organized by the GAA Foundation and hosted by the European Cultural Centre as part of the 2018 Venice Architecture Biennale. David Kenyon, Andrew Chardain, AIA, Brian J. Mac, FAIA, Jeff McBride, AIA, Jeff Kumuda, Tim Hennessey and Peter Abiles.

BIRDSEYE

WWW.BIRDSEYEVT.COM

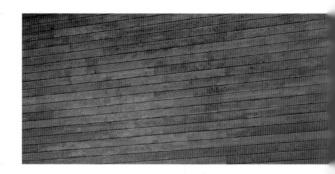

Birdseye est un studio de design renommé de Richmond, dans le Vermont, offrant des services en architecture et architecture d'intérieur pour une clientèle privée. Fondé en 1997 par l'architecte principal, Brian J. Mac, FAIA, ce cabinet est spécialisé dans le design résidentiel personnalisé. Visible dans tout le Nord-Est américain, leur travail reflète une évaluation permanente et le raffinement de l'art et l'artisanat, profondément ancré dans la tradition du bâtiment de la région. Les concepts de design découlent d'une exploration réfléchie, itérative, à la fois du littéral et de l'abstrait. Birdseye a obtenu plusieurs prix de design internationaux et de nombreuses distinctions de l'Institut américain des architectes, à la fois au niveau local et régional. Ce cabinet participe à l'exposition architecturale de 2018, *Time Space Existence* organisée par la Fondation GAA et accueillie par le Centre culturel européen dans le cadre de la Biennale d'architecture de Venise. David Kenyon, Andrew Chardain, AIA, Brian J. Mac, FAIA, Jeff McBride, AIA, Jeff Kumuda, Tim Hennessey et Peter Abiles.

Birdseye è un rinomato studio di design con sede a Richmond, Vermont, impegnato in servizi di architettura e design di interni per clienti privati. Fondato nel 1997 dall'architetto capo Brian J. Mac, FAIA, lo studio è specializzato nel design residenziale personalizzato. Presente in tutta l'America nord-orientale, il lavoro dello studio riflette una valutazione e un perfezionamento continui del binomio arte + artigianato, saldamente radicati nella tradizione edilizia del luogo. I concetti del design derivano da un'esplorazione attenta e iterativa delle idee di letterale e astratto. Birdseye ha ricevuto numerosi premi internazionali per il design e onorificenze da parte dell'American Institute of Architects, a livello sia locale sia regionale. Lo studio è tra i partecipanti della mostra di architettura Time Space Existence 2018, organizzata dalla Fondazione GAA e ospitata dal Centro Culturale Europeo all'interno della Biennale di Architettura di Venezia, edizione 2018. David Kenyon, Andrew Chardain, AIA, Brian J. Mac, FAIA, Jeff McBride, AIA, Jeff Kumuda, Tim Hennessey e Peter Abiles.

LIFT HOUSE

WOODSHED

Lift House is sited on a narrow property adjacent to a ski trail on a Vermont mountainside. The footprint of the house is boomerang-shaped to fit the landscape, with sleeping spaces below and social spaces on the top floor to maximize views.

The reverse-living arrangement is emphasized in the materiality and massing of the house. The lower volume is a heavy, corten steel-clad form which anchors the house to the sloping mountainside and supports the floating form above. Entrances are nearly invisible. The upper form is a visually larger, cedar-clad cantilevered structure. The wood extends out to create a substantial hooded opening and covered deck for this floor, providing both shelter from the weather and privacy for the residents. This expansive form is composed of generous social spaces and large glazed walls with panoramic views of the ski trail and Vermont landscape.

LIFT HOUSE

© Erica Allen Studio

Lift House est située sur une propriété étroite bordant une piste de ski sur une montagne du Vermont. L'empreinte de la maison a la forme d'un boomerang afin de s'inscrire dans le paysage, les espaces nuit étant au-dessous et les espaces partagés à l'étage supérieur pour profiter avantageusement des vues.

L'agencement des pièces contraire à l'habitude est accentué par la matérialité et les masses de l'habitation. Le volume inférieur est une masse lourde bardée d'acier Corten qui ancre la maison au flanc de la montagne et soutient la forme suspendue qui la surplombe. Les entrées sont presque invisibles. Le volume supérieur est une structure visuellement plus vaste, recouverte d'un bardage en cèdre. Le bois s'étend jusqu'à créer une ouverture encapuchonnée et un deck couvert pour cet étage, procurant à la fois un abri vis-à-vis des intempéries et une intimité pour ses résidents. Cette vaste forme est composée d'espaces communs généreux et de grands murs vitrés offrant une vue panoramique sur la piste de ski et le paysage du Vermont.

Lift House è situata su una piccola proprietà confinante con una pista da sci su un versante montuoso del Vermont. La pianta della casa è a forma di boomerang per adattarsi al paesaggio; la zona notte è al piano di sotto, mentre gli spazi in comune sono posti al piano superiore per godere al meglio dei panorami.

La sistemazione inversa degli spazi abitativi è esaltata dalla materialità e dalla volumetria della casa. Il volume inferiore è massiccio, rivestito di acciaio corten, e àncora la casa al versante scosceso, sostenendo al contempo la forma fluttuante del piano superiore. Le entrate sono quasi invisibili. Il volume superiore è una struttura visibilmente più grande, rivestita in cedro e con elementi a sbalzo. Il legno si estende per creare un'importante apertura nascosta e un ponte coperto per questo piano, offrendo agli abitanti rifugio dalle intemperie e privacy. La forma estesa racchiude ampi spazi per la socializzazione e grandi pareti vetrate che aprono la vista sulla pista da sci e sul panorama del Vermont.

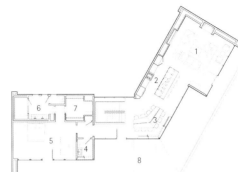

1. Living room
2. Kitchen
3. Dining
4. Powder room
5. Master bedroom
6. Master bathroom
7. Master closet
8. Covered porch

Second floor plan

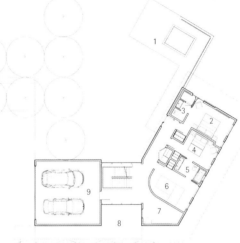

1. Hot tub / Outdoor patio
2. Guest bedroom
3. Guest bathroom
4. Bedroom
5. Bathroom
6. Bedroom
7. Entry vestibule
8. Covered walkway entry
9. Garage

First floor plan

1. Ski-in / Ski-out room
2. Kids room
3. Bathroom
4. Exercise room
5. Storage

Basement plan

0   10m

This project is conceptually inspired by the vernacular woodshed, a familiar and iconic element in the Vermont landscape. It is nestled in the foothills of the Green Mountains in Pomfret, Vermont. Sited on a steeply sloping and heavily wooded site, Woodshed is both a guest house and entertainment space for the main residence down the road. It is composed of two asymmetric gable roof forms, akin to the traditional woodshed, connected by a central entryway. The western, public elevation presents the continuous, wood textured wall that evokes the expressive, scrim wall of a traditional woodshed. The project purposefully projects a minimal familiar elevation to the non-view, public road side and an engaging, contemporary open elevation to the private hillside. This side opens to the views with a glass façade that invites the landscape, exterior retaining walls and terrace spaces into the structure.

WOODSHED

© Jim Westphalen

Ce projet est inspiré conceptuellement par la vernaculaire cabane en bois, élément familier et iconique du paysage du Vermont. Il est niché au pied des *Green Mountains* de Pomfret, au Vermont. Situé sur une forte pente et un emplacement très boisé, *Woodshed* est à la fois une maison d'hôtes et un espace de divertissement pour la résidence principale du bas de la rue. Il est composé de deux formes asymétriques de toitures à deux versants rappelant la cabane en bois traditionnelle, reliées par une entrée centrale. L'élévation ouest, publique, présente un mur continu, texturé, en bois qui évoque celui, expressif et ajouré, des cabanes en bois traditionnelles. Ce projet exhibe à dessein une élévation minimale familière du côté route, sans vue, et un côté ouvert engageant et contemporain donnant sur le versant privé de la colline. Ce côté s'ouvre sur la vue avec une façade qui invite le paysage, les murs porteurs extérieurs et les terrasses dans la structure.

Questo progetto si ispira concettualmente al capanno vernacolare, elemento familiare e iconico nel panorama del Vermont. Si trova in una posizione protetta, ai piedi della Green Mountains, nel comune di Pomfret, Vermont. L'area è caratterizzata da pendii scoscesi e ricoperti di boschi; Woodshed è sia una guest house sia uno spazio ricreativo per la residenza principale che si trova in fondo alla strada. Il complesso si compone di due volumi asimmetrici con tetto a capanna, simili al tradizionale capanno locale, collegati da un ingresso centrale. Il prospetto pubblico orientato verso occidente presenta la parete continua di legno che rievoca la trama particolare dei capanni tradizionali. Il progetto prevede intenzionalmente un piccolo prospetto familiare sul lato chiuso alla vista dalla strada, e un interessante prospetto in chiave moderna che dà sul pendio privato. Questo lato si apre al panorama tramite una facciata in vetro che si integra con il paesaggio, con i muri di sostegno e gli spazi terrazzati.

Section

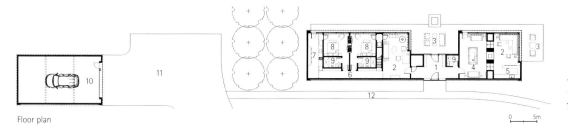

Floor plan

1. Entry
2. Living
3. Outdoor living
4. Entertainment
5. Bar
6. Hall
7. Kitchenette
8. Bedroom
9. Bathroom
10. Garage
11. Driveway
12. Walkway

0   5m

More than two decades since its founding in Jackson Hole, Wyoming, the firm has evolved but it essentials remain unchanged. The projects are recognizable: thoughtful, innovative, and refined in their details. A collaborative process enables the studio to engage clients and therefore the portfolio is loaded with a diverse set of designs each responsive to a particular set of conditions. The power of landscape, the quality of light and the simple honesty of vernacular architecture influence the work. Each endeavour is guided with the firm's philosophy in mind – inspired by place. Since its inception in 1992, the Jackson studio has grown to accommodate a staff of more than 40 led by principals John Carney, Eric Logan, Kevin Burke and Andy Ankeny. In 2017 they opened a full-service design studio in Bozeman.

CARNEY
LOGAN BURKE

WWW.CLBARCHITECTS.COM

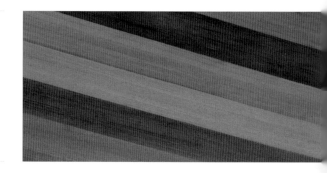

Plus de deux décennies après sa création à Jackson Hole, dans le Wyoming, cette compagnie a évolué mais reste fondamentalement la même. Les projets en sont reconnaissables : bien pensés, novateurs, et raffinés dans leurs moindres détails. Un fonctionnement collaboratif permet à ce cabinet d'impliquer les clients et par conséquent son portefeuille de travaux est empli d'un éventail varié de designs, chacun répondant à un ensemble particulier de conditions. Le pouvoir du paysage, la qualité de la lumière et la simple honnêteté de l'architecture vernaculaire en influencent le travail. Chaque projet est mené en gardant à l'esprit la philosophie de la compagnie : inspiré par le lieu. Depuis sa création en 1992, le studio de Jackson s'est agrandi pour accueillir plus de 40 employés menés par ses directeurs John Carney, Eric Logan, Kevin Burke et Andy Ankeny.

A più di due decenni dalla sua fondazione a Jackson Hole, Wyoming, lo studio si è evoluto, ma la sua essenza è rimasta invariata. I progetti sono riconoscibili: attenti, innovativi e rifiniti nei minimi dettagli. Il processo collaborativo fa sì che lo studio coinvolga i clienti. La gamma di servizi viene così arricchita di progetti con finalità diverse, ognuno rispondente a un particolare insieme di condizioni. L'energia del paesaggio, la qualità della luce e la semplice onestà dell'architettura vernacolare influenzano il lavoro. Ogni impegno è illuminato dalla filosofia dello studio: ispirarsi al contesto. Sin dal suo avvio, nel 1992, lo studio di Jackson è cresciuto fino ad accogliere uno staff di oltre 40 elementi, guidati da John Carney, Eric Logan, Kevin Burke e Andy Ankeny. Nel 2017 hanno aperto uno studio di design full-service a Bozeman.

BUTTE RESIDENCE   HOME RANCH WELCOME CENTER   RCR COMPOUND

The 38-acre site for this family compound including a main house and art barn is located on an extraordinary site perched above Jackson, Wyoming. The site overlooks the confluence of the Snake and Gros Ventre Rivers and commands panoramic views of the mountains beyond. The design was driven by the desire to capitalize on the potential of this spectacular site while weaving the architecture of the compound into the topography. In addition, the owner, a collector of contemporary art and sculpture, wanted the buildings to show a character and materiality that respect western tradition but with clean, contemporary, light-filled spaces. By breaking up the program into a series of volumes that range across the site, individual spaces open to varied views and access points. Gently curving roof forms separately capture public and private functions within the residential program. The roof profile mimics the soft shape of the butte and provides a series of broad protective canopies, which become a symbol for shelter in the harsh western landscape.

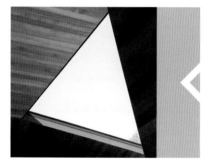

BUTTE RESIDENCE

© Matthew Millman, Paul Warchol

Le site de 15 hectares attribué à ce domaine familial comportant une habitation principale et une grange consacrée à l'art se trouve sur une parcelle extraordinaire dominant la ville de Jackson dans le Wyoming. Il donne sur la confluence entre *Snake River* et *Gros Ventre River* et offre une vue panoramique sur les montagnes à l'horizon. Le design a été motivé par le désir d'exploiter le potentiel de ce site spectaculaire tout en incorporant l'architecture de cet ensemble dans la topographie du lieu. De plus, le propriétaire, collectionneur d'art et de sculpture, voulait que les bâtiments aient un caractère et une matérialité qui respecte la tradition de l'Ouest américain mais avec des espaces purs, contemporains, remplis de lumière. En séparant le programme architectural en une série de volumes qui s'étendent sur tout le site, des espaces individuels ouvrent sur des vues et des points d'accès variés. Des formes de toitures aux courbes légères séparent les fonctions publiques des privées dans le cadre du programme résidentiel. Le profil du toit rappelle la forme souple de la butte et offre une série de larges voûtes protectrices, devenant ainsi des symboles du refuge dans le rude paysage de l'ouest américain.

I 15 ettari che ospitano questa residenza di famiglia, composta dalla casa principale e da una dépendance con opere d'arte, si trovano sopra il centro abitato di Jackson, Wyoming. L'area sovrasta la confluenza dei fiumi Snake e Gros Ventre, offrendo panorami delle montagne che si estendono oltre quel punto. Il progetto è stato ispirato dal desiderio di fare tesoro del potenziale offerto da quest'area spettacolare, intrecciando la costruzione nella topografia. Inoltre, il proprietario, collezionista di arte e scultura contemporanee, aveva chiesto che il complesso mostrasse un carattere e una materialità rispettose della tradizione occidentale, ma con spazi puliti, moderni, inondati di luce. Suddividendo il progetto in una serie di volumi disposti all'interno dell'area, gli spazi individuali si aprono a panorami e punti di accesso diversi. La forma del tetto, dolcemente curva, separa le funzioni pubbliche da quelle private all'interno della residenza. Il profilo del tetto imita le dolci forme della montagna e offre una serie di ampie tettoie di protezione che divengono simbolo di rifugio sicuro nell'aspro paesaggio occidentale.

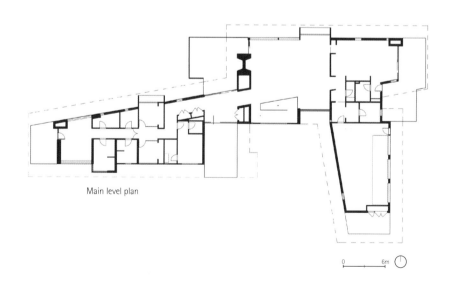

Main level plan

0   6m

Demarcating the northern entrance to Jackson, Wyoming's historic downtown, the Home Ranch Welcome Center serves as a community hub for both residents and visitors alike. A forest of log columns introduces visitors to an interactive display that informs and educates on the natural splendor that Jackson, Wyoming is uniquely centered within. These columns support a large canted roof with glass clerestory that tilts up to the southern light and the omnipresent backdrop of downtown Jackson, Snow King Mountain.

The building replaces an existing well-worn public restroom facility and updates this function with a robust material palette to provide increased longevity. A LEED Gold rating has been received in accordance with the Town's sustainability initiative. Directly adjacent to the primary parking lot for visitors arriving from points north to experience downtown Jackson, the Home Ranch Center also serves as a transportation hub for the valley's public transit service.

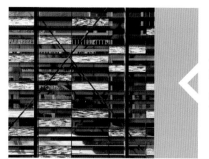

HOME RANCH WELCOME CENTER

© Matthew Millman, Paul Warchol

Délimitant l'entrée nord du centre historique de Jackson, dans le *Wyoming*, le *Home Ranch Welcome Center* sert de carrefour communautaire pour les résidents comme les visiteurs. Une forêt de colonnes en bois introduit les visiteurs à une exposition interactive qui informe et éduque sur les splendeurs naturelles qui entourent la ville et font sa particularité unique. Ces colonnes soutiennent un immense toit en biseau portant des persiennes de bois qui pivotent vers la lumière du sud et le décor omniprésent du centre de Jackson, *Snow King Mountain*.

Ce bâtiment remplace une ancienne installation sanitaire très usée et reprend cette fonction avec une palette de matériaux robuste pour lui permettre de durer. Une certification LEED Gold lui a été accordée dans le cadre de l'initiative de la ville pour la durabilité. Directement adjacent au parking principal pour les visiteurs arrivant des points nord pour visiter le centre de Jackson, le *Home Ranch Center* sert aussi de carrefour routier pour les services de transport public de la vallée.

Posto all'ingresso settentrionale di Jackson, cittadina storica del Wyoming, l'Home Ranch Welcome Center funge da community hub per gli abitanti del luogo e i turisti. Una foresta di pilastri ricavati accoglie il visitatore a una presentazione interattiva che informa e istruisce sulle meraviglie naturali al centro delle quali sorge Jackson, Wyoming. I pilastri sostengono un ampio tetto inclinato, dotato di un claristorio che si innalza fino a catturare la luce da sud e l'immancabile scenario che fa da sfondo a Jackson, Snow King Mountain.

Il complesso sostituisce il vecchio e fatiscente stabilimento dei bagni pubblici e aggiorna la sua funzione scegliendo materiali robusti che ne aumentino la longevità. Il progetto ha ricevuto la certificazione LEED Gold in base all'iniziativa per la sostenibilità della Città. Direttamente adiacente alla principale area di parcheggio per i visitatori che arrivano da nord per ammirare la cittadina di Jackson, l'Home Ranch Center funge anche da snodo per il servizio di trasporto pubblico della vallata.

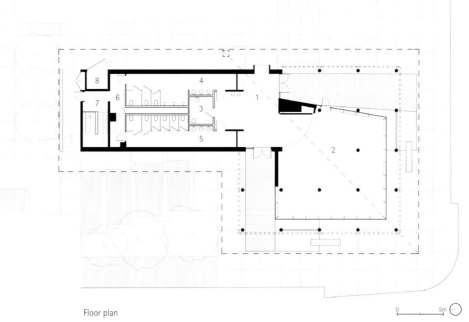

Floor plan

0   5m

1. Entry
2. Exhibit
3. Family bathroom
4. Men's bathroom
5. Women's bathroom
6. Storage
7. Stair
8. Recycling

The art collector clients for RCR relocated to this rural setting where they desired a house that capitalized on the characteristics of the extraordinary site and created an appropriate setting for the display and enjoyment of their collection. This 9,000-square-foot house is organized as a series of connected building forms that surround an elevated courtyard. Approach to the compound leads through the meadow, gradually rising to an entry court at the base of the butte. Primary living and entertaining spaces reside at a level above the meadow to access distant views and warm south light. The living spaces flow seamlessly onto a covered exterior porch that cantilevers above the meadow. In contrast, a library space is positioned on the intimate courtyard nestled into the base of the butte. The master bedroom and meditation area reside in a separate building connected by a glass bridge creating a completely private zone for quiet and contemplation. The walnut flooring of the upper level cascades down a stairway to the meadow level that accommodates a den, exercise room and art storage.

RCR COMPOUND

© Matthew Millman

Ces clients de RCR collectionneurs d'art se sont relogés dans ce cadre rural où ils désiraient une maison qui exploiterait les caractéristiques de ce site extraordinaire et créerait un lieu approprié pour exposer leur collection et en disposer. Cette maison de près de 850 mètres carrés est organisée en une série de bâtiments qui entourent une cour surélevée. L'abord du domaine fait traverser la prairie, remontant progressivement vers une cour d'entrée à la base de la butte. Les espaces principaux de vie et de réception se trouvent sur un niveau au-dessus de la prairie pour accéder aux points de vue sur le lointain et à la chaleureuse lumière du sud. Les espaces à vivre se succèdent dans un flot continu jusqu'à un porche extérieur couvert en porte-à-faux au-dessus de la verdure. Un espace bibliothèque est positionné sur la cour intime blottie à la base de la butte. La chambre principale et l'espace dédié à la méditation sont situés dans un bâtiment séparé relié par un pont de verre, créant une zone complètement privée pour le calme et la contemplation. Le sol en noyer à l'étage supérieur descend en cascades par un escalier jusqu'au niveau de la prairie qui accueille un petit salon, une salle de gym et une pièce pour entreposer des œuvres d'art.

I clienti del progetto RCR, collezionisti d'arte, si sono trasferiti in questo ambiente rurale nel momento in cui hanno deciso di fare tesoro delle straordinarie caratteristiche del luogo e creare un ambiente adeguato per disporre e godersi la loro collezione. La casa da 836 metri quadrati è organizzata in una serie di volumi collegati tra loro, che circondano una corte sopraelevata. L'accesso alla residenza conduce attraverso il prato, salendo gradualmente fino a raggiungere l'entrata ai piedi della collina. I principali spazi abitativi e ricreativi sono di un livello più alti del prato, per godere dei panorami e della calda luce da sud. Gli spazi abitativi scorrono senza interruzione lungo un portico esterno coperto che sporge al di sopra del prato. Lo spazio dedicato alla biblioteca è posizionato nella corte raccolta, inserita ai piedi della collina. La camera da letto padronale e la zona data alla meditazione si trovano in un edificio separato, accessibile tramite un ponte di vetro, che crea uno spazio privato per il silenzio e la contemplazione. Il pavimento in noce del piano superiore si srotola lungo una scala fino al livello del prato, che accoglie uno studio-rifugio, una palestra e un magazzino per le opere d'arte.

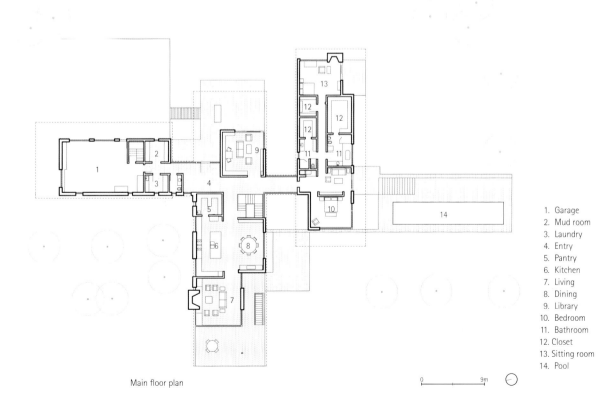

Main floor plan

1. Garage
2. Mud room
3. Laundry
4. Entry
5. Pantry
6. Kitchen
7. Living
8. Dining
9. Library
10. Bedroom
11. Bathroom
12. Closet
13. Sitting room
14. Pool

0   9m

Lindsay + Kerry Clare are an award-winning husband and wife architectural team —collaborating to produce outstanding buildings. Clare Design has been producing architectural projects for nearly 40 years including a diverse range of houses and major urban and public buildings consistently acknowledged for their rare combination of design excellence and high-level environmental performance. "The Clares' ideas about experiencing natural light and ventilation are merged with their ideas about typology. They fuse ideas about type and climate into building form." Their buildings allow occupants to engage with architecture and the world outside, reinforcing the essential connection with place.

CLARE DESIGN

WWW.CLAREDESIGN.COM.AU

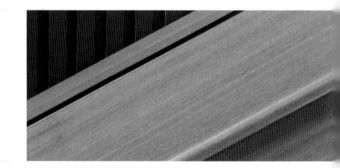

Lindsay + Kerry Clare représentent une équipe architecturale primée formée par un couple dont la collaboration produit des bâtiments remarquables. Clare Design produit des projets architecturaux depuis presque 40 ans parmi lesquels un éventail divers de maisons et des constructions urbaines et publiques majeures ont toujours confirmé leur association exceptionnelle d'excellence dans le design et leur niveau élevé de performance environnementale. « Les idées des Clare sur l'usage de la lumière et l'aération naturelles sont combinées à leur conception de la typologie. Ils fusionnent des réflexions sur le type et le climat sous forme de bâti. » Leurs constructions permettent aux occupants d'entrer en relation avec l'architecture et le monde extérieur, renforçant la connexion essentielle avec le lieu.

Lindsay + Kerry Clare formano un team di architetti pluripremiati, e sono marito e moglie. Scopo della loro collaborazione è creare edifici straordinari. Clare Design realizza progetti architettonici da quasi 40 anni, progetti che includono una varietà di case ed edifici urbani e pubblici di grande importanza, ampiamente riconosciuti per la loro rara combinazione di eccellenza del design e prestazioni ambientali di alto livello. "Le idee dei Clare sull'uso della luce e della ventilazione naturali si fondono con i loro concetti di tipologia. Quello che fanno è combinare le idee su tipo e clima traducendole in forma architettonica". Le loro costruzioni permettono agli occupanti di interagire con l'architettura e il mondo esterno, rafforzando il legame intrinseco con il posto.

DOCKLANDS LIBRARY

Site plan

The City of Melbourne engaged Clare Design to undertake studies in Melbourne's newly developed Docklands identifying opportunities for cultural and community interventions to moderate the impact of large developments and instil a fine urban grain and sense of place. The Docklands Library, which also contains within it a series of other public functions, is part of the City of Melbourne's strategy of inserting or updating public libraries across the municipality. For Rob Adams, director of city design at City of Melbourne, each library was to be an urban exemplar, not just in terms of knitting together context, morphology and public space, but also in pushing the boundaries of technology, especially with regard to responsible environmental design. Sited on a heritage timber wharf the Library is built in CLT and Glulam to achieve a building 30% lighter than one of traditional construction. Users consistently report the Library as providing an inspiring place to learn, study and work.

DOCKLANDS LIBRARY

© Emma Cross, Dianna Snape, John Gollings

La ville de Melbourne a engagé Clare Design pour entreprendre des études dans le quartier fraîchement développé des Docklands identifiant les opportunités d'interventions culturelles et communautaires visant à modérer l'impact de grands ensembles et à insuffler un fin maillage urbain et un sentiment d'appartenance au lieu. La bibliothèque des Docklands, qui contient également une série d'autres fonctions publiques, fait partie de la stratégie d'insertion et de réfection de bibliothèques publiques dans cette municipalité. Pour Rob Adams, directeur du design urbain de la ville de Melbourne, chaque bibliothèque devait être un exemple d'urbanisme, non seulement pour ce qui est de tisser des liens entre contexte, morphologie et espace public, mais aussi en vue de repousser les frontières technologiques, en particulier dans le design environnemental responsable. Situé sur un quai classé en structure de bois, la bibliothèque est construite en CLT et en lamellé-collé pour aboutir à un bâtiment plus léger de 30 % par rapport à une construction traditionnelle. Les usagers parlent fréquemment de ce lieu comme d'un lieu inspirant pour apprendre, étudier et travailler.

La Città di Melbourne ha chiesto a Clare Design di condurre uno studio sui suoi Dockland di più recente sviluppo, per individuare eventuali opportunità di interventi culturali e comunitari che potessero attutire l'impatto delle grandi strutture e instaurare una fine grana urbana e il senso del luogo. La Docklands Library, che include al suo interno una serie di funzioni pubbliche altre, è parte della strategia della Città di Melbourne di inserire nuove biblioteche pubbliche al suo interno, o riqualificare quelle già esistenti. Per Rob Adams, direttore della progettazione urbana della Città di Melbourne, ogni biblioteca doveva essere un esempio urbano, non soltanto in termini di connessione tra contesto, morfologia e spazio pubblico, ma anche come ridefinizione degli orizzonti tecnologici, con particolare riferimento alla progettazione ambientale responsabile. Ubicata su un antico molo in legno, la Library è costruita in CLT e legno lamellare incollato per ottenere un edificio il 30% più leggero rispetto a una costruzione tradizionale. L'opinione unanime degli utenti dipinge la Library come un posto perfetto dove imparare, studiare e lavorare.

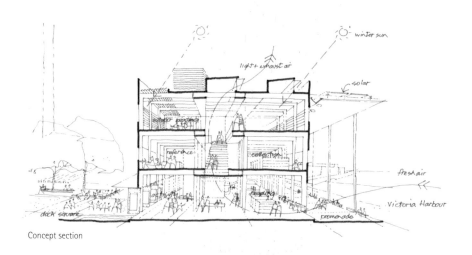

Concept section

Second floor plan

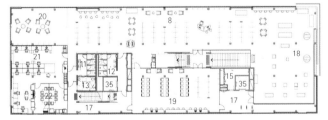

First floor plan

1. Entry	18. Gallery
2. Main entry foyer	19. Quiet study
3. Information	20. Reading lounge
4. Cafe	21. Staff room
5. Cafe store	22. Staff meeting room
6. Foyer	23. Music and media
7. Activity room	24. Design lab
8. Library	25. Gameplay
9. Children's library	26. Makerspace
10. After hours	27. Recording room
entry/exit	28. Editing suite
11. Female WC	29. Practice room
12. Male WC	30. Multi-purpose
13. Accessible WC	31. Community space
14. Baby change	32. Performance space
15. Services	33. Meeting room
16. Store	34. Terrace
17. Lobby	35. Lift

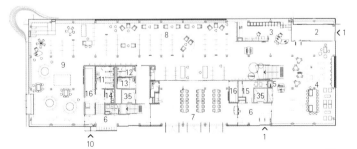

Ground floor plan

Nils Finne, AIA, is principal of the award-winning FINNE Architects in Seattle. His residential work has been widely published locally and nationally in over 100 books and magazines. FINNE Architects has been recognized as one of the best Seattle design firms by local and national media. In addition to architecture, Nils has been involved in the design and fabrication of more than 80 pieces of furniture, lighting and hardware. He is known for highly crafted, sustainable, modern residential architecture. Prior to founding FINNE Architects in 1991, Nils was a Senior Associate at Richard Meier and Partners, and served as Project Architect for the $350 million Getty Museum, approximately one-third of the $1 billion Getty Center complex in Los Angeles. Nils received a M.Arch degree in from Harvard Graduate School of Design in 1980. He has been practicing sustainable design for over 25 years, and is a member of the U.S. Green Building Council.

FINNE ARCHITECTS

WWW.FINNE.COM

Nils Finne, AIA, est président de FINNE Architects, cabinet primé de Seattle. Son travail résidentiel a fait l'objet de publications dans plus de 100 livres et magazines locaux et nationaux. FINNE Architects est reconnu comme étant l'une des meilleures compagnies de design de Seattle par les médias locaux et nationaux. En plus de l'architecture, Nils a été impliqué dans le design et la fabrication de plus de 80 articles de mobilier, d'éclairage et d'équipement. Il est connu pour une architecture résidentielle moderne, durable, et extrêmement élaborée. Avant de fonder FINNE Architects en 1991, Nils était Associé principal chez Richard Meier & Partners, et a travaillé comme architecte de projet pour le *Getty Museum*, projet de 350 millions d'USD, approximativement équivalent à un tiers du complexe de 1 milliard du *Getty Center* à Los Angeles. Il a obtenu son diplôme d'architecture à l'École de design de Harvard en 1980. Il pratique le design durable depuis plus de 25 ans, et fait partie du *Green Building Council* des États-Unis.

Nils Finne, AIA, è a capo del premiato studio FINNE Architects di Seattle. I suoi lavori di edilizia residenziale sono stati pubblicati a livello locale e nazionale in oltre 100 libri e riviste del settore. FINNE Architects è stato riconosciuto dai media locali e nazionali come uno dei migliori studi di design di Seattle. Non solo architettura: Nils ha dato il proprio contributo al design e alla realizzazione di oltre 80 componenti di arredo, illuminazione e hardware. È rinomato per la sia architettura residenziale moderna, sostenibile e di altissima qualità artigianale. Prima di fondare lo studio FINNE Architects nel 1991, Nils è stato Senior Associate di Richard Meier and Partners e Architetto progettista del Getty Museum, opera del valore di 350 milioni di dollari, rappresentante circa un terzo del complesso da 1 miliardo di dollari Getty Center di Los Angeles. Nils ha conseguito la laurea M.Arch nel 1980, presso la Harvard Graduate School of Design. Opera nell'architettura sostenibile da più di 25 anni ed è membro dell'U.S. Green Building Council.

THE DESCHUTES HOUSE   VENICE HOUSE   ELLIOTT BAY HOUSE

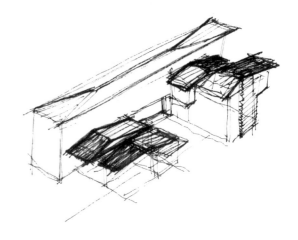

The Deschutes House is a river house, located on the Deschutes River in Bend, Oregon. The house wraps around a south-facing, grassy courtyard, with dramatic 2nd story spaces cantilevered toward the river. The main living space is completely transparent to the river on one side and to the courtyard on the other side, providing two entirely different views. The living ceiling plane has CNC-milled wood ceiling panels, inspired by landscape morphology. The house is clad with two different types of siding: tightly spaced red cedar and corrugated metal siding. The warm tones of the wood contrast with the metal siding and metal roofing. The fireplace chimney is clad in Montana ledgestone. The house has many sustainable building features: 2x8 construction (40% greater insulation value); large glass areas to provide natural lighting and ventilation; roof overhangs for sun and snow protection; metal siding for durability; and radiant floor heating. The house also has solar hot water panels.

THE DESCHUTES HOUSE

© Benjamin Benschneider

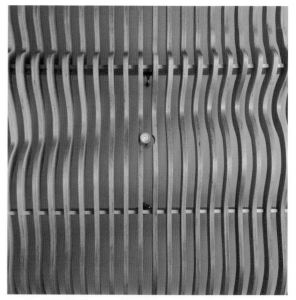

La Deschutes House est une maison située sur la *Deschutes River* à Bend, en Orégon. Cette maison entoure une cour engazonnée orientée au sud comportant des espaces impressionnants à deux étages en porte-à-faux vers la rivière. L'espace à vivre principal est complètement transparent du côté de l'eau et, à l'opposé, du côté de la cour, ce qui permet de bénéficier de deux vues complètement différentes. Le plan du plafond du séjour est composé de panneaux de bois découpés au laser inspirés par la morphologie du paysage. La maison est bardée de deux types de revêtements : l'un recouvert de cèdre rouge en lames à joints serrés et l'autre de tôle ondulée. Les tons chaleureux du bois contrastent avec le revêtement et la couverture métalliques. La cheminée est garnie de *ledgestone* du Montana. La maison est dotée de nombreuses caractéristiques du bâtiment durable : une construction en 2 x 8 (pour une valeur d'isolation supérieure) ; de larges surfaces vitrées pour procurer aération et lumière naturelles ; des surplombs de toiture pour se protéger du soleil et de la neige ; des revêtements en métal pour la durabilité ; et du chauffage radiant au sol. Cette maison est également équipée de panneaux solaires pour l'eau chaude.

Deschutes House è una casa sul fiume Deschutes, a Bend, nello stato dell'Oregon. La casa si sviluppa intorno a una corte ricca di vegetazione e rivolta a sud, ed è caratterizzata dai bellissimi ambienti del secondo piano, che si sporgono verso l'acqua del fiume. Lo spazio abitabile principale offre due panorami completamente differenti: uno spalancato sul fiume, l'altro sulla corte. Il ripiano a soffitto della zona living è composto da pannelli di legno fresato a CNC, ispirati alla morfologia del paesaggio. La casa presenta due diversi tipi di rivestimento, uno in cedro rosso disposto fittamente disposto e uno in lamiera ondulata. I toni caldi del legno contrastano con quelli freddi del rivestimento e del tetto metallici. Il comignolo del camino è rivestito in pietra agglomerata del Montana. In materia di sostenibilità, l'edificio è molto ben strutturato: Elementi 2x8 (valore di isolamento maggiore del 40%), grandi vetrate per favorire illuminazione e ventilazione naturali, sporgenze a protezione da sole e neve, rivestimenti in metallo per la durabilità, pavimento radiante. La casa è dotata anche di pannelli solari per l'acqua calda.

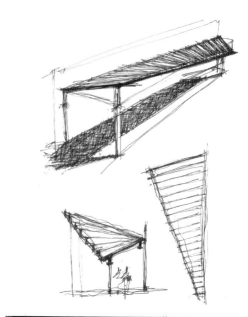

The Venice House is a garden sanctuary on a narrow lot in Los Angeles. The house consists of a series of folded roof planes and a collage of textured metal and wood exterior surfaces. Most of the house has been placed on the eastern side of the lot, making a garden on the western side. The wood living pavilion projects into the garden space, with a soaring hyperbolic paraboloid roof formed by exposed Douglas fir beams. A pool has been placed directly outside the living area, allowing this prominent part of the house to be mirrored by water. Oversized 8-ft by 10-ft sliding glass doors open directly from the dining area to the pool. Interior finishes are simple, with rift-sawn white oak cabinets and floors combined with white plaster walls. A custom steel light fixture hangs over the quartz kitchen island and cast-glass breakfast counter. The house is highly energy-efficient, with deep roof overhangs, natural lighting and ventilation, LED lighting, and drought-tolerant landscaping.

VENICE HOUSE

© Tom Bonner

La Venice House est un jardin sanctuaire situé sur une parcelle étroite à Los Angeles. Cette maison est composée d'une série de plans de toiture pliés, d'un collage de métal texturé et de surfaces extérieures en bois. La majorité de cette habitation a été placée sur le côté est de la parcelle, créant un jardin du côté ouest. Le pavillon séjour en bois se projette dans l'espace jardin avec son toit paraboloïde vertigineux formé par des poutres apparentes en pin douglas. Une piscine a été placée directement à l'extérieur du séjour, permettant à cette partie essentielle de la maison de se refléter dans l'eau. Des portes coulissantes surdimensionnées de 2,50 mètres par 3 ouvrent directement de l'espace repas sur la piscine. Les finitions intérieures sont simples, avec des placards et des sols en chêne blanc débité sur quartiers associés à des murs blancs en plâtre. Une lampe en acier faite sur-mesure est suspendue au-dessus de l'îlot de cuisine en quartz et du bar en verre moulé pour petit-déjeuner. La maison a une grande efficacité énergétique, avec ses surplombs de toit, son aération et son éclairage naturels, son éclairage LED, et son jardin paysagé pour résister à la sécheresse.

Venice House è un rifugio verde sito su uno stretto terreno in Los Angeles. La casa si sviluppa in una serie di tetti a falde e un collage di superfici esterne in metallo goffrato e legno. La porzione più consistente della casa è stata costruita sulla parte orientale dell'area; il giardino occupa la parte occidentale. Il padiglione abitabile in legno si proietta nello spazio del giardino, con un tetto paraboloide iperbolico composto da travi a vista in abete di Douglas. Subito fuori dall'area living, una piscina riflette questa parte sporgente della casa. Grandi porte scorrevoli a vetri, da 2,5 x 3 m, si aprono direttamente dalla zona pranzo sulla piscina. Le finiture interne sono semplici, con credenze e pavimenti in quercia bianca segata radialmente, abbinati a pareti intonacate di bianco. Una lampada personalizzata in acciaio pende sulla cucina a isola in quarzo e sul banco da colazione in vetro colato. È una casa ad alta efficienza energetica, con profonde sporgenze delle coperture, illuminazione e ventilazione naturali, luci a LED e vegetazione resistente alla siccità.

The Elliott Bay House is located in Seattle, on a site facing Puget Sound. The house has a south-facing court-yard containing a reflecting pool with two "floating" basalt boulders. The reflecting pool in the courtyard gathers all the roof drainage, with the living room roof downspout providing a 10-ft waterfall. The courtyard is intimate, in contrast to the sweeping views of Puget Sound on the west side of the living space. The wood beams in the living space change pitch dramatically along the length of the room. Modern craft is prevalent in the house. A water jet-cut steel fence and gate lead to the house entry. Exterior siding is custom-milled red cedar. The steel and wood stairs have water jet-cut steel railings with a hand-drawn pattern. The beech interior cabinets have a CNC-milled pattern called "imaginary landscape." The house is highly energy efficient and heavily insulated, with a radiant hydronic heat system. Large glass areas provide natural lighting and ventilation.

ELLIOTT BAY HOUSE

© Benjamin Benschneider

Elliott Bay House est une maison située à Seattle, sur un site donnant sur le détroit de Puget. Elle comporte une cour orientée au Sud contenant une piscine miroir dotée de deux rochers de basalte « flottant » sur l'eau. Celle-ci récupère toutes les eaux de pluie du toit, la descente de gouttière du toit du séjour procurant une chute d'eau de 3 mètres. La cour est intime, contrastant avec les vues panoramiques sur le détroit de Puget à l'ouest du séjour. Les poutres en bois de l'espace de vie changent radicalement d'inclinaison dans la longueur de la pièce. Une clôture métallique et un portail découpés au jet d'eau mènent à l'entrée de la maison. Le revêtement extérieur est en cèdre rouge usiné sur mesure. Les marches en acier et bois sont équipées de rampes en acier découpé au jet d'eau portant un motif dessiné à main levée. Les placards intérieurs en hêtre portent un motif appelé « paysage imaginaire », gravé au moyen d'une machine à commande numérique. Cette maison est très efficace au niveau énergétique, fortement isolée et dotée d'un système de chauffage hydronique radiant. De grandes surfaces vitrées procurent aération et lumière naturelles.

Elliott Bay House si trova a Seattle, su un'area che guarda lo Stretto di Puget. La casa è impreziosita da una corte rivolta a sud, con uno specchio d'acqua riflettente, sul quale "galleggiano" due massi di basalto. Il bacino raccoglie l'acqua piovana dal tetto, trasformata in una cascata alta 3 metri dalla grondaia della zona living. La corte è intima e raccolta, in contrasto con l'ampio panorama dello Stretto di Puget sul lato occidentale dello spazio abitabile. Le travi in legno dello spazio abitabile variano visibilmente lungo lo sviluppo della stanza. Nella casa prevale l'artigianato moderno. Una recinzione e un cancello in acciaio tagliato a getto d'acqua conducono all'ingresso della casa. Il rivestimento esterno è costituito da cedro rosso lavorato su disegno del cliente. Le scale in acciaio e legno hanno ringhiere in acciaio tagliato a getto d'acqua, con motivo disegnato a mano. L'arredamento interno in faggio è impreziosito da un motivo fresato a CNC, denominato "paesaggio immaginario." È una casa ad alta efficienza energetica, con un ottimo grado di isolamento e un sistema di riscaldamento radiante idronico. Ampie zone vetrate offrono illuminazione e ventilazione naturali.

Flansburgh Architects is a Boston-based architecture firm recognized as a leader in the planning and design of educational and cultural facilities in the US and abroad. The firm's innovative designs have won over 125 national and regional design awards from industry peers and educators. Flansburgh emphasizes a cost-effective, environmentally responsive approach to design. The firm's designs provide an uplifting, stimulating environment characterized by flexible spaces, state of the art equipment, generous daylight, effective ventilation, comfortable furniture, harmonious colors, appropriate scale, appealing character, and natural materials. Flansburgh believes that the quality of our surroundings has a direct influence on the quality of our lives, whether, on campus, in the workplace, at a show, or in the public realm. In that sense, design is all encompassing, ranging from the functional and environmental performance of a building to a concern for its physical and cultural context.

FLANSBURGH
ARCHITECTS

WWW.FLANSBURGH.COM

Flansburgh Architects est un bureau d'architecture basé à Boston reconnu comme leader dans la planification et le design d'équipements pédagogiques et culturels aux Etats-Unis et à l'étranger. Ses designs novateurs lui ont valu plus de 125 récompenses nationales et régionales dans le domaine du design. Flansburgh tient à une approche du design rentable, écologiquement responsable. Les designs de ce cabinet créent un environnement stimulant caractérisé par les espaces souples, un équipement de pointe, un éclairage naturel abondant, une aération efficace, un mobilier confortable, des couleurs harmonieuses, une échelle adaptée, un caractère attirant et des matériaux naturels. Flansburgh croit que la qualité de notre environnement influe directement sur notre qualité de vie, que ce soit sur les campus, au travail, au spectacle, ou dans le domaine public. En ce sens, le design est universel, allant de la performance fonctionnelle et environnementale d'un bâtiment au souci de son contexte physique et culturel.

Flansburgh Architects è uno studio di architettura con sede a Boston, riconosciuto come leader nella pianificazione e progettazione di edifici dati all'istruzione e alla cultura sia negli USA che all'estero. Gli innovativi progetti dell'azienda sono stati premiati con oltre 125 riconoscimenti nazionali e regionali. Flansburgh promuove un approccio alla progettazione efficiente in termini di costi e responsabile verso l'ambiente. I progetti dello studio offrono un ambiente confortante e stimolante, caratterizzato da spazi flessibili, apparecchi all'avanguardia, abbondante illuminazione, ventilazione efficace, arredamenti confortevoli, colori armoniosi, dimensioni a misura d'uomo, carattere seducente e materiali naturali. Flansburgh crede che la qualità dell'ambiente circostante abbia un'influenza diretta sulla qualità della nostra vita, a scuola come sul posto di lavoro, mentre assistiamo a uno spettacolo o frequentiamo luoghi pubblici. In questo senso, il progetto è globalizzante, e si estende dalla prestazione funzionale e ambientale di un edificio fino all'interesse per il suo contesto fisico e culturale.

HAWAII PREPARATORY ACADEMY
ENERGY LAB

INDIAN MOUNTAIN SCHOOL
CREATIVE ARTS CENTER

JACOB'S PILLOW DANCE
PERLES FAMILY STUDIO

The first building in the world to meet the Living Building Challenge, the new Energy Lab at Hawaii Preparatory Academy functions as a zero-net-energy, fully sustainable. Given the favorable Hawaiian climate and the building's dramatic hillside setting, direct connections to the outdoors are enhanced via operable glass doors. An entry court is located to the east, a large teaching porch opens directly south, and a wind-sheltered court to the west extends into a covered outdoor classroom, which uses the trunk of a native Hawaiian Ohia tree as a supporting column. Board formed concrete, glued laminated structure and wood decking recall the architecture of the school's original campus. Polycarbonate skylights, interior roller shades and wood sun screens all work together to introduce, reflect and control natural day light. These components were strategically employed to satisfy foot candle minimums, tackle glare, and enhance views, resulting in a pleasantly lit interior environment.

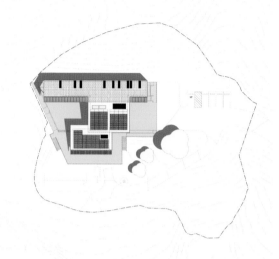

Site plan

0   30m

HAWAII PREPARATORY ACADEMY
ENERGY LAB

© Matthew Millman

Le premier bâtiment du monde à répondre au *Living Building Challenge*, le nouveau *Energy Lab* de la *Hawaiian Preparatory Academy* fonctionne en tant que bâtiment à énergie zéro, complètement durable. Étant donné le climat favorable hawaiien et l'emplacement magnifique du bâtiment à flanc de colline, des liaisons directes avec l'extérieur sont mises en valeur par le biais de portes vitrées ouvrantes. Une cour d'entrée est située à l'est, un large porche ouvre directement sur le sud, et une cour abritée du vent à l'ouest se prolonge en une salle de classe extérieure couverte, qui se sert du tronc d'un ohia, arbre hawaiien, comme colonne porteuse. Béton imprimé imitation bois, structure en lamellé collé et terrasse en bois rappellent l'architecture du campus d'origine de l'école. Les fenêtres de toit en polycarbonate, les stores et les écrans en bois s'allient pour introduire, réfléchir et contrôler la lumière naturelle du jour. Ces composantes ont été employées de façon stratégique pour répondre aux exigences minimales de pieds bougies, éviter les reflets, et mettre en valeur les vues, ce qui a donné un environnement intérieur à l'éclairage agréable.

Prima costruzione al mondo a soddisfare i criteri del protocollo Living Building Challenge, la nuova Energy Lab at Hawaii Preparatory Academy funziona a energia netta pari a zero, ed è completamente sostenibile. Forti del favorevole clima hawaiano e della magnifica posizione collinare, i collegamenti con l'esterno sono valorizzati dalle porte a vetri azionabili. Una corte d'ingresso è posizionata sul lato orientale, un ampio portico/area per l'insegnamento si apre direttamente verso sud e una corte riparata dal vento a ovest si estende fino a un'aula all'aperto dotata di copertura, dove un grande tronco di ohia delle Hawaii fa da colonna portante. Calcestruzzo formato in assi, struttura in legno lamellare incollato e ballatoi in legno richiamano l'architettura del campus originale della scuola. Lucernari in policarbonato, tende a rullo per gli interni e schermi solari in legno collaborano per lasciare entrare, riflettere e controllare la luce naturale. Tutti gli elementi sono strategicamente organizzati per soddisfare i requisiti minimi di illuminazione, contrastare il riverbero ed esaltare la vista, dando come risultato un ambiente interno piacevolmente illuminato.

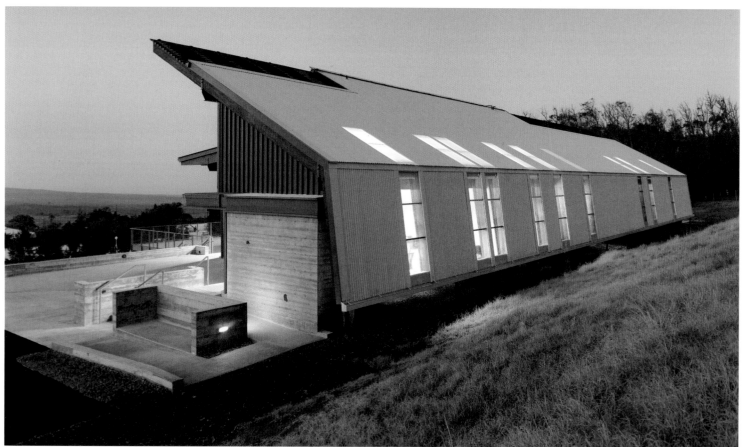

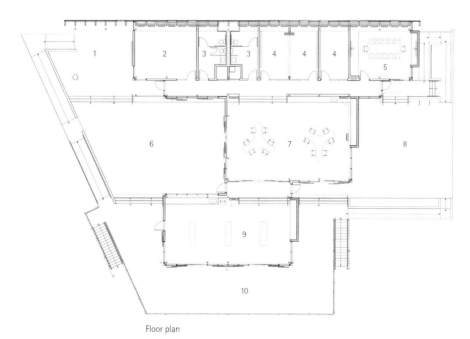

Floor plan

1. Outdoor classroom
2. Monitoring lab
3. Bathroom
4. Project room
5. Conference room
6. Courtyard
7. Workstations
8. Wind terrace
9. Workshop
10. Sun deck

Located on a 600-acre campus in western Connecticut, the site sits on a gently sloping hillside directly adjacent to existing campus buildings with views of Indian Mountain to the west. The school's 8,750-sq. ft. Creative Arts Center integrates visual arts, music and science through collaborative, cross-disciplinary, project-based learning. The design recalls a traditional New England barn with a sloped tin roof, exposed timber and board, and batten siding; however, the angled glass walls slice open the barn-like building to expose the beauty of the interior wood structure and to take advantage of dramatic mountain views to the west. Solid areas of the exterior envelope are clad with board and batten, and insulated glass is attached directly to glued laminated timbers at glass areas. Painted concrete floors, exposed metal strapping, exposed steel fasteners accentuate the wood structure by conveying an honesty of expression and integration of structure, materiality and architecture.

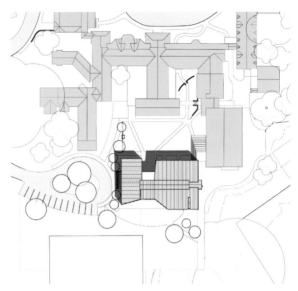

Site plan

INDIAN MOUNTAIN SCHOOL
CREATIVE ARTS CENTER

© Robert Benson

Situé sur un campus de 243 hectares à l'ouest du Connecticut, ce site est installé sur la pente douce d'une colline directement adjacente aux bâtiments existants du campus, avec des vues sur les *Indian Mountains* à l'ouest. Le Centre d'arts créatifs de cette école, d'une surface de 813 mètres carrés, réunit les arts visuels, la musique et les sciences par le biais d'un enseignement collaboratif, inter-disciplinaire et axé sur le projet. Ce design rappelle une ancienne grange traditionnelle avec son toit de zinc incliné, ses poutres et planches apparentes, et son bardage de tasseaux ; cependant, les murs vitrés des angles découpent ce bâtiment qui évoque une grange pour révéler la structure en bois de l'intérieur et profiter de la vue magnifique sur la montagne à l'ouest. Des zones massives de l'enveloppe extérieure sont bardées de planches et de tasseaux, et un vitrage isolé est relié directement au lamellé collé au niveau des zones vitrées. Les sols en béton peint, les bandes métalliques et les fixations en acier apparentes font ressortir la structure en bois en apportant une honnêteté d'expression et l'intégration d'une structure, d'une matérialité et d'une architecture.

Ubicato su un campus da 243 ettari nel Connecticut occidentale, l'edificio poggia su un fianco collinare dolcemente scosceso, vicino alle preesistenti sedi del campus, aprendosi sulla Indian Mountain verso ovest. La scuola misura 8.750 metri quadrati. Il Creative Arts Center include arti visive, musica e scienze attraverso un metodo di insegnamento collaborativo, interdisciplinare e basato sul progetto. Il progetto richiama un tradizionale fienile del New England, con tetto spiovente in stagno, legno e assi a vista e rivestimenti a listelli; le pareti angolari in vetro aprono l'edificio-fienile per esporre la bellezza della struttura interna in legno e per godere appieno dei panorami montani verso ovest. Le zone piene dell'involucro esterno sono rivestite con assi e listelli, mentre il vetro isolante delle finestre è fissato direttamente al legno lamellare incollato. I pavimenti in calcestruzzo dipinto, le cinghie di metallo esposte e i fissaggi in acciaio anch'essi a vista esaltano la struttura in legno trasmettendo lealtà di espressione e integrazione della struttura, della materialità e dell'architettura.

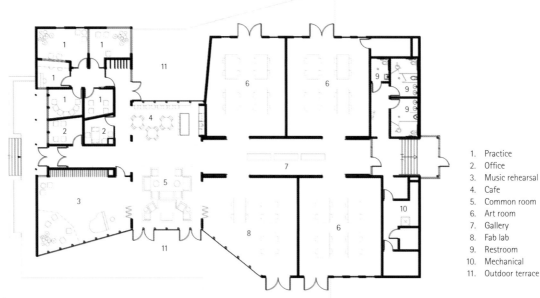

1. Practice
2. Office
3. Music rehearsal
4. Cafe
5. Common room
6. Art room
7. Gallery
8. Fab lab
9. Restroom
10. Mechanical
11. Outdoor terrace

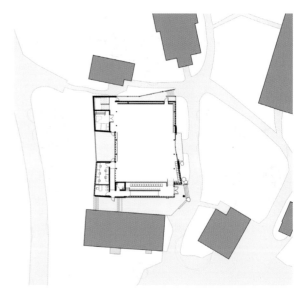

Site plan

The site is a steeply sloping, thickly-wooded, 0.25-acre parcel nestled between two existing, wood-framed studio buildings to its north and south. Featuring a 3,500-sq.ft. dance floor, the 7,500-sq.ft. new Perles Family Studio draws students, performers, and visitors into a close and intimate space. It exudes an organic, casual modesty in keeping with the site's origin as a farm, while echoing the revered Berkshire landscape. Emblematic of straightforward simplicity and New England frugality, the design employs clerestories and cupolas to control natural light and airflow and uses carefully chosen building materials to minimize sound overflow between the studios. Integral to this design vision are standing seam metal roofing, cedar siding and decking, and interior pine paneling that give the new building its distinct visual character. The new studio serves as a multi-functional venue for teaching, rehearsals, and informal performances, in addition to hosting visiting artists.

JACOB'S PILLOW DANCE
PERLES FAMILY STUDIO

© Robert Benson

Ce site consiste en une parcelle en pente raide, couverte d'une dense forêt, d'un peu plus de 1000 mètres carrés nichée entre deux bâtiments existants à cadre en bois au nord et au sud. Avec sa piste de danse de 325 mètres carrés, le nouveau *Perles Family Studio* attire étudiants, interprètes et visiteurs dans un espace fermé et intime. Il évoque une modestie informelle et organique en accord avec l'origine agricole du site, tout en se faisant l'écho du paysage bien-aimé du Berkshire. Emblématique de la simplicité directe et de la frugalité de la Nouvelle Angleterre, ce design emploie des persiennes et des coupoles pour contrôler la lumière et l'aération naturelles et utilise des matériaux de construction choisis avec soin pour minimiser les nuisances sonores entre les studios. La couverture en métal à joints debout, les bardages et les decks en cèdre, et le lambris intérieur en pin font partie intégrante de ce design et donnent au nouveau bâtiment son caractère visuel distinct. Ce nouveau studio sert de salle multi-fonctions pour l'enseignement, les répétitions, et les représentations informelles, en plus de permettre d'héberger les artistes de passage.

Una ripida pendenza, densamente boscosa, con un appezzamento da 0,25 acri incastonato tra due preesistenti edifici-studio con strutture in legno posti ai lati nord e sud. Con la sua pista da ballo di 3.500 metri quadrati, il nuovo Perles Family Studio di 7.500 metri quadrati attira studenti, performer e visitatori nel suo spazio intimo e coperto. Il posto emana una modestia organica e casuale, in armonia con la funzione originale di fattoria, e richeggia il venerato paesaggio del Berkshire. Emblema della semplicità diretta e della frugalità tipiche del New England, il progetto impiega claristori e cupole per controllare la luce naturale e la ventilazione, e utilizza materiali da costruzione scelti con cura per ridurre al minimo il traboccare dei suoni da uno studio all'altro. Fondamentali per questo punto di vista della progettazione sono la copertura in lamiera aggraffata, i fianchi e i ballatoi in cedro e i pannelli interni in pino che conferiscono all'edificio un carattere visivo distinto. Il nuovo studio funge da centro multifunzionale per l'insegnamento, le prove e le performance informali, oltre a ospitare gli artisti in visita.

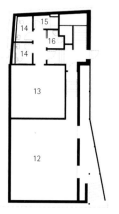

Basement plan

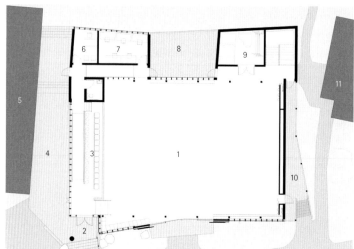

First floor plan

1. Studio floor
2. Visitor entrance
3. Seating
4. Visitor porch
5. Sommers studio
6. Office
7. Group office
8. Dancer's porch
9. Storage
10. Crossover porch
11. Rose studio
12. Mechanical room
13. Dressing/storage
14. Restroom
15. Shower
16. Janitor's closet

Frank la Rivière, Architects is a multi-disciplinary and internationally oriented design practice based in Tokyo working in the field of architecture and interior design through to graphic and product design. Led by ir Frank la Rivière (The Netherlands Utrecht, 1961) who studied architecture and interior design at Delft University of Technology (Master's degree first class honors). Our design approach is centered on the research into the relation between People, Object and Space, from which a specific design strategy emerges for each project. With recurring themes such as lightness, transparency, continuous flow of space and trueness to the nature of the materials used we aim to create agreeable habitable environments, responsive to the needs of its occupiers. Our designs are subtracted from the cultural, social and programmatic conditions, while the characteristics of the climate, the site restrictions, as well as the available techniques are major sources of inspiration.

FRANK LA RIVIÈRE, ARCHITECTS

WWW.FRANK-LA-RIVIERE.COM

Frank la Rivière, Architects est un cabinet de design multi-disciplines et international basé à Tokyo qui œuvre dans le domaine de l'architecture et du design d'intérieur jusqu'au design graphique et de produits.. Dirigé par Frank La Rivière (Utrecht, Pays-Bas, 1961) qui a étudié l'architecture et le design d'intérieur à l'Université de technologie de Delft (Mastère, mention très honorable). Notre approche du design se concentre sur la recherche orientée sur la relation entre les personnes, l'objet et l'espace, dont se dégage une stratégie spécifique de design à chaque projet. Avec des thèmes récurrents comme la légèreté, la transparence, la fluidité de l'espace et le respect de la nature des matériaux utilisés, nous cherchons à créer des environnements habitables agréables, adaptés aux besoins de leurs occupants. Nos designs puisent dans les conditions culturelles, sociales et de programmation tandis que les caractéristiques du climat, les restrictions du site, ainsi que les techniques disponibles sont des sources majeures d'inspiration.

Frank la Rivière, Architects è uno studio di design multidisciplinare e internazionale con sede a Tokyo, la cui attività si estende dai campi dell'architettura e dell'interior design fino a quello del design grafico e del prodotto. A capo dello studio, Frank la Rivière (Utrecht, Paesi Bassi, 1961), laureato in architettura e design di interni all'Università Tecnica di Delft (laurea specialistica ottenuta con il massimo dei voti). Il nostro approccio alla progettazione si basa sulla ricerca all'interno della relazione tra Persona, Oggetto e Spazio; relazione da cui emerge una strategia progettuale specifica per ogni opera. Attraverso temi ricorrenti come leggerezza, trasparenza, flusso continuo dello spazio e lealtà alla natura dei materiali scelti, vogliamo creare ambienti abitabili piacevoli, che rispondano alle esigenze dei loro occupanti. I nostri progetti nascono dalle condizioni culturali, sociali e programmatiche; fattori come le caratteristiche climatiche, le limitazioni del luogo e le tecniche a nostra disposizione costituiscono una grande fonte di ispirazione.

N-HOUSE

S-HOUSE

Constructed on a deep plot of land in Aomori prefecture, the linearity of this private residence is articulated by means of transition zones. In the longitudinal direction a vista knits together the living room, dining area, the Japanese room and the garden in one view. All these major spaces are articulated by "in-between zones" placed in lateral direction which create a sense of varying depth and visual measurability. These transition zones do not only separate they also connect, being part of the circulation and giving access to the functions in the service zone. The openness can be moderated by opening or closing sliding doors. By using color difference (orange concrete formwork plywood against birch plywood) in the floor and changes in the ceiling the spaces are determined. Add to this the clarity of the module (900 x 900 mm) used to give rhythm to the materials and reinforcing the optical measurability of the spatial distances

N-HOUSE

© Frank la Rivière

Construite sur une parcelle encaissée de la préfecture d'Aomori, cette résidence privée est articulée dans sa linéarité par le biais de zones de transition. Dans la direction longitudinale une perspective couvre le séjour, le coin repas, le salon japonais et le jardin en un seul regard. Tous ces principaux espaces sont articulés par des « zones transitoires » placées dans le sens de la largeur, ce qui crée une impression de profondeurs variables et de mesurabilité. Ces zones de transition, non contentes de séparer, servent également de lien, participant à la circulation et donnant accès aux fonctions de la zone de service. L'ouverture peut en être modérée en ouvrant et fermant les portes coulissantes. L'utilisation de différentes couleurs (contreplaqué de béton formé orange contre contreplaqué de bouleau) sur le sol et les changements au niveau du plafond déterminent les espaces. Il faut ajouter à cela la clarté du module (900 x 900 mm) utilisé pour rythmer les matériaux et renforcer la mesurabilité optique des distances dans l'espace.

Costruita su una profonda area edificabile nella prefettura di Aomori, questa residenza privata presenta una linearità che si articola attraverso zone di transizione. Il senso longitudinale collega il soggiorno, la zona pranzo, la camera in stile giapponese e il giardino in un unico colpo d'occhio. Questi spazi di grande importanza si articolano in "zone intermedia" poste in direzione laterale, che creano un senso di profondità variabile e misurabilità visiva. Le zone di transizione non soltanto separano, ma collegano, essendo parte del percorso e fornendo l'accesso alle utilità della zona di servizio. Gli spazi aperti possono essere modulati attraverso l'apertura e la chiusura di porte scorrevoli. È la differenza di colore (pannelli arancione in compensato da cassaforma contro pannelli in compensato di betulla) nel pavimento e le variazioni del soffitto a determinare gli spazi. A questo si aggiunga la purezza del modulo (900 x 900 mm) utilizzato per dare ritmo ai materiali e rafforzare la misurabilità ottica delle distanze spaziali.

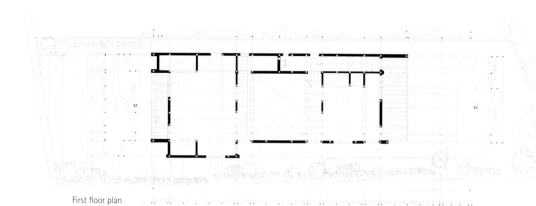

First floor plan

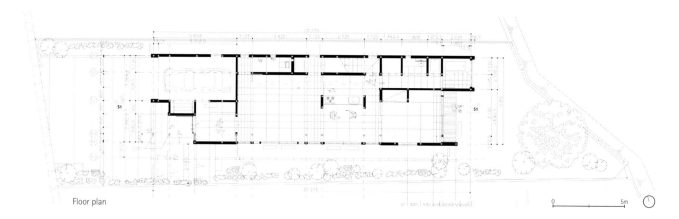

Floor plan

0 _____ 5m

North elevation

East elevation

South elevation

West elevation

0   5m

0   5m

The client sought to build a one-story house full of light whilst protective of privacy. In response a square open plan lay-out was designed of 9.1 x 9.1 m based on the Japanese module for timber structures with high side windows, at each corner of the house, in order to create an interior with abundant natural light. These four 2.7 m high windows with light catchers, look like Four Ears against the sky, while the central roof light works as a sundial. The open plan guarantees the feeling of lightness, because all four high-side windows remain visible, but also allows for an even distribution of cooled or heated air. The zoning is designed for flexibility. A storage unit between the living zone and the sleeping zone together with two columns compose of a square in the center of the house purposed to be the living area, the core of daily life. All functions are grouped around this central square. The sleeping zone spans the whole width of the house and can be freely separated into three smaller zones by the movable wardrobes.

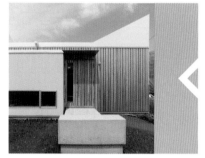

S-HOUSE

© Frank la Rivière

Le client cherchait à construire une maison à un étage remplie de lumière mais préservant son intimité. Pour y répondre, un plan d'étage ouvert de 9,1 x 9,1 m a été conçu, basé sur le module japonais de structures en bois avec de hautes fenêtres latérales sur chaque angle de la maison, afin de créer un intérieur baigné de lumière naturelle. Ces quatre fenêtres de 2,7 m équipées de récupérateurs de lumière ressemblent à quatre oreilles dressées vers le ciel, tandis que la lumière centrale du toit fonctionne comme un cadran solaire. Le plan ouvert y garantit un sentiment de légèreté, car les quatre fenêtres du côté haut restent visibles, mais permettent également une répartition harmonieuse de l'air climatisé ou chauffé. La répartition des zones est pensée pour la flexibilité. Un module de rangement entre l'espace à vivre et le coin nuit ainsi que deux colonnes composent un carré au centre de la maison conçu pour être la zone séjour, le cœur de la vie quotidienne. Toutes les fonctions sont regroupées autour de ce carré central. L'espace nuit s'étend sur toute la largeur de l'habitation et peut être séparé librement en trois zones plus réduites par le biais de penderies mobiles.

South-east facade

Il cliente voleva una casa a un piano, inondata dalla luce ma al contempo rispettosa della privacy. La risposta è stata la progettazione di un open space quadrato di 9,1 x 9,1 m, basato sul modulo giapponese per le strutture in legno, con alte finestre laterali in ogni angolo della casa, in modo da creare un ambiente pieno di luce naturale. Queste quattro finestre alte 2,7 m con attira-luce sembrano quattro orecchi rivolti verso il cielo, mentre la luce che filtra dal tetto centrale funge da meridiana. L'open space garantisce la sensazione di leggerezza, poiché tutte e quattro le alte finestre rimangono visibili, e consente anche un'ottimale distribuzione di aria calda o fredda. La suddivisione in zone è progettata pensando alla flessibilità. Una unità ripostiglio tra il soggiorno e la zona notte compone, insieme a due pilastri, un quadrato al centro della casa, pensato per essere l'area soggiorno, fulcro della vita quotidiana. Tutte le funzioni sono raggruppate intorno a questo quadrato centrale. La zona notte si estende per tutta l'ampiezza della casa e può essere facilmente suddivisa in tre aree più ridotte spostando gli armadi mobili.

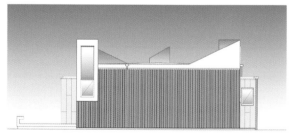

North-east facade

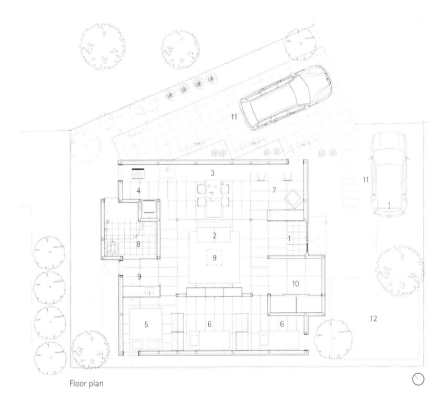

Floor plan

1. Entrance
2. Living
3. Dining
4. Kitchen
5. Parents sleeping area
6. Childs sleeping area
7. Study area
8. Bathroom & toilet
9. Washing room
10. Japanese room
11. Parking
12. Garden

Jeff Svitak Inc. was founded in 2012, focusing primarily on architectural design, while simultaneously integrating both real estate development and general contracting into its practice. The company prides itself on creating unique and inspired human environments that engage with the senses of the user. While each project has it's own individual inspiration and concept, Svitak believes heavily in the role of spatial organization and it's influence on human emotions. By intimately studying this relationship, Jeff Svitak Inc. looks to enhance the emotional quality of it's buildings inhabitants; thoughtfully integrating aspects of privacy and intimacy within the interior environment, connecting exterior living spaces, and inviting an overall sense of community through crafted and welcoming public and circulatory spaces.

JEFF SVITAK

WWW.JEFFSVITAK.COM

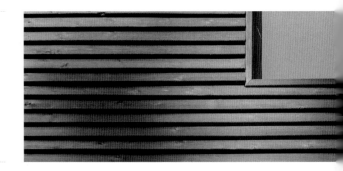

Jeff Svitak Inc. a été fondé en 2012, principalement axé sur le design architectural, tout en intégrant simultanément la promotion immobilière et entrepreneuriat général à son portefeuille. Cette société s'enorgueillit de créer des environnements humains uniques et inspirés qui font appel aux sens de l'usager. Alors que chaque projet possède sa propre inspiration et son propre concept, Svitak croit fermement au rôle de l'organisation de l'espace et de son influence sur les émotions humaines. En étudiant intimement cette relation, Jeff Svitak Inc. cherche à faire ressortir la qualité émotionnelle des habitants de ses constructions ; en intégrant respectueusement des aspects privatifs et intimes de l'environnement intérieur, en reliant les espaces extérieurs, et en invoquant un sentiment global de communauté par le biais d'espaces publics et circulatoires élaborés et accueillants.

Jeff Svitak Inc. nasce nel 2012, e si concentra soprattutto sulla progettazione architettonica, integrando simultaneamente nella propria attività sia la costruzione di immobili sia l'attività di general contractor. L'azienda si vanta di creare ambienti umani unici e ispirati, che dialogano con i sensi di chi li occupa. Sebbene ogni progetto abbia un'ispirazione e un concetto unici, Svitak crede fermamente nel ruolo dell'organizzazione spaziale e nell'influenza di questa sulle emozioni umane. Attraverso uno studio approfondito di questo rapporto, Jeff Svitak Inc. vuole esaltare la qualità emotiva delle sue costruzioni e di chi le abita, integrando attentamente aspetti di privacy e intimità all'interno dell'ambiente abitativo, collegando spazi da vivere all'esterno, incoraggiando un generale senso di comunità e accogliendo spazi pubblici dati al passaggio delle persone.

REDWOOD HOUSE

A house and studio nestled into a unique canyon running through the city of San Diego. The concept was to diffuse the division between canyon and house, so that the two flow together seamlessly. Instead of a blunt massing object between the street and the canyon, the house is divided into separate massing elements, which allow the canyon to enter into the spaces of the house and studio through a slim courtyard element. The house is accessed across a floating steel bridge, and through a sliding cedar door that begins the reveal moments and windows into the canyon setting beyond, although limited and controlled. From there the user travels through the various spaces of the house as the canyon unveils itself if full form. The living room space is a cantilevered room floating within the natural elements of the canyon. The circulation flows inside and out, access to the bedrooms is through an outdoor vestibule and then into a soft wood box where trees are the only visual element. The basement has another outdoor private access and is utilized as the architect's office and studio.

REDWOOD HOUSE

© Onnis Luque, Tomoko Matsubayashi

Cette maison équipée d'un atelier est nichée dans un canyon exceptionnel traversant la ville de San Diego. Le concept en était d'atténuer la division entre le canyon et la maison, de sorte qu'il puisse y avoir une continuité entre les deux. Au lieu d'être une masse franche entre la rue et le canyon, cette habitation est séparée en blocs distincts, ce qui permet au canyon de pénétrer dans les espaces de la maison et de l'atelier par le biais d'une étroite cour. On accède à la maison par un pont d'acier suspendu, et par une porte coulissante en cèdre qui entame les moments de révélation, et des fenêtres donnant sur le canyon au-delà, quoiqu'il soit limité et contrôlé. A partir de ce point, l'usager voyage à travers les différents espaces à mesure que le canyon se dévoile dans toute son intégralité. L'espace séjour est une pièce en porte-à-faux en suspension au cœur des éléments naturels du canyon. La circulation est fluide à l'intérieur comme à l'extérieur, l'accès aux chambres se faisant par un vestibule extérieur puis un module en bois tendre où les arbres constituent le seul élément visuel. Le rez-de-chaussée possède un autre accès privé et sert de bureau et d'atelier à l'architecte.

Casa e studio incastonati in un canyon unico nel suo genere, che attraversa la città di San Diego. L'idea era attutire la divisione tra canyon e casa, in modo che i due elementi potessero scorrere insieme senza interruzione. Al posto di un unico esplicito oggetto tra la strada e il canyon, la casa è suddivisa in elementi separati, che consentono allo stesso canyon di insinuarsi negli spazi tra casa e studio attraverso la snella corte.I Si accede alla casa tramite un ponte galleggiante in acciaio e una porta scorrevole di cedro, che inizia a rivelare l'ambiente e le finestre che affacciano sul canyon sottostante, anche se in modo cauto, controllato. Da lì in poi, il visitatore viaggia attraverso i diversi spazi della casa, e poco a poco il canyon si rivela in tutta la sua bellezza. Lo spazio living è una camera aggettante che galleggia in mezzo agli elementi naturali del canyon. Il passaggio è scorrevole, l'accesso alle camere da letto avviene tramite un vestibolo esterno e quindi in un piccolo ambiente in legno dove l'unico elemento visivo è costituito da alberi. Il piano interrato è dotato di un altro accesso indipendente, ed è utilizzato come ufficio e studio dell'architetto.

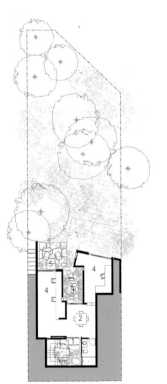

Basement floor plan

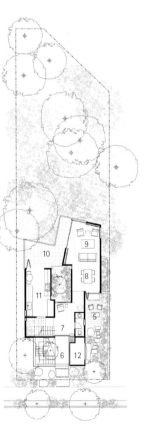

First floor plan

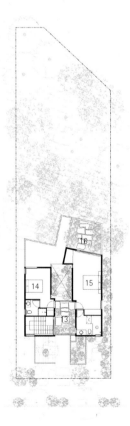

Second floor plan

1. Entry courtyard
2. Meeting room
3. Courtyard
4. Studio
5. Patio
6. Bridge
7. Entry
8. Dinning
9. Living
10. Deck
11. Kitchen
12. Storage
13. Outdoor vestibule
14. Bedroom
15. Master bedroom
16. Green roof patio

0   6m

Our work is distinguished by a commitment to architecture's expression of the human experience, and is built on a combined love of craft with an appreciation of technology to develop projects respectful of their environment with expressive architectural details that celebrate building materials and the construction trades. A passion for the stories of people's lives and the role of buildings in them drives our work. By building on existing traditions and historic vernacular, we not only contribute to the continuum of the human experience, but also work to keep the history of a place alive and evolving. Our keen understanding of community as a living and changing organism has led us to focus on projects that enhance the communal experience and expand the role of architecture in public life. Coming full circle and connecting physically to what came before, we feel an obligation to re-use and recycle materials. We strive to use each material in the best way possible, both in craft and detail.

JOHN GRABLE
ARCHITECTS

WWW.JOHNGRABLE.COM

Notre travail se distingue par un engagement à l'expression de l'expérience humaine par l'architecture et se construit sur l'association de notre amour du travail artisanal et de notre appréciation de la technologie pour développer des projets respectueux de leur environnement avec des détails architecturaux qui célèbrent les matériaux de construction et les savoir-faire du bâtiment. C'est la passion pour les récits de vie des personnes et le rôle que les bâtiments y jouent qui guide notre travail. En s'appuyant sur les traditions existantes, nous contribuons à la continuité de l'expérience humaine et aussi à œuvrer pour le maintien en vie de l'histoire d'un lieu et pour son évolution. Notre compréhension aiguë de la communauté en tant qu'organisme vivant et évolutif nous a mené à nous concentrer sur des projets qui mettent en valeur l'expérience commune et élargissent le rôle de l'architecture dans la vie publique. La boucle étant bouclée, nous connectant physiquement à ce qui nous a précédé, nous ressentons l'obligation de réutiliser et de recycler les matériaux. Nous nous efforçons d'utiliser chaque matériau de la meilleure façon possible.

Il nostro lavoro si distingue per l'impegno nell'espressione dell'esperienza umana attraverso l'architettura, e poggia sull'unione tra l'amore per l'artigianato e l'apprezzamento della tecnologia, allo scopo di sviluppare progetti rispettosi dell'ambiente, con dettagli architettonici espressivi che celebrino i materiali da costruzione e le professionalità coinvolte. La passione per le storie delle persone e il ruolo che in esse giocano gli edifici è ciò che muove il nostro lavoro. Costruendo su tradizioni esistenti e aree dall'importanza storica, non solo partecipiamo alla continuità dell'esperienza umana, ma aiutiamo a mantenere viva e in evoluzione la storia di un luogo. La profonda comprensione da parte nostra della comunità come organismo vivente e in continuo mutamento ci ha portati a concentrarci su progetti che esaltino l'esperienza comunitaria e ampliino il ruolo dell'architettura nella vita pubblica. Volendo chiudere il cerchio e collegarci fisicamente a quel che c'era prima, sentiamo l'obbligo di riutilizzare e riciclare i materiali. Ci impegniamo a utilizzare ogni materiale nel miglior modo possibile, in qualsiasi applicazione.

MUSIC BOX

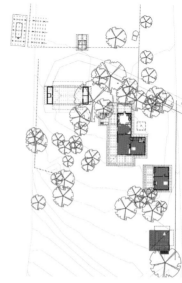

Site plan

0   30m

Sited directly off the banks of the West Sister Creek, this floating structure was erected to serve as a sanctuary for both music and health. The program with-in the single volume space is two-fold, acting both as a yoga studio as well as a music room. The floor boards were constructed using Cypress Planks while the walls were constructed with reclaimed Sinker Cypress panels, both materials were selected to resonate with the scenic cypress trees which rise from the nearby creek banks. The location of the piano, bounded by the dual Sinker Cypress walls and Cypress Floor Boards, produces perfect acoustics by directing and amplifying the performance rendering the space ideal for intimate concerts or for personal musical reflection. The roof deck is 1 ½" Southern Yellow Pine Structural Deck, which allowed for the generous rafter spacing, exposed at the interior the deck is stained with a light-blue stain reminiscent of typical Ranch Porches of the area.

MUSIC BOX

© Dror Baldinger, John Grable Architects

Située directement sur le bord du West Sister Creek, cette structure en suspension a été érigée pour servir de sanctuaire orienté à la fois sur la musique et sur la santé. Le programme architectural à l'intérieur de cet espace comporte deux volets, ce volume servant à la fois de salle de yoga et de salle de musique. Les lames du parquet ont été fabriquées en planches de cyprès tandis que les murs ont été construits en panneaux de cyprès « trempé », ces deux matériaux ayant été sélectionnés pour être en résonance avec les cyprès pittoresques des rives du ruisseau voisin. L'emplacement du piano, circonscrit par les murs et les planchers en cyprès, produit une acoustique parfaite en dirigeant et amplifiant la performance, rendant cet espace idéal pour des concerts intimes ou pour une réflexion musicale personnelle. La terrasse du toit est un deck structurel en pin jaune du sud 1 W, ce qui a permis l'espacement généreux entre les lames ; apparent à l'intérieur, celui-ci est teint en bleu clair, rappelant les porches typiques des ranchs des environs.

Ubicata sulle rive del West Sister Creek, fiume del Texas, questa struttura galleggiante è stata realizzata per fungere da santuario della musica e della salute. Lo scopo del volume interno è duplice: sala di yoga e sala della musica. La pavimentazione è composta da tavole di cipresso, le pareti sono costruite con pannelli di cipresso rigenerato. Entrambi i materiali sono stati selezionati per armonizzarsi con i suggestivi alberi di cipresso che impreziosiscono le vicine rive del fiume. La posizione scelta per il pianoforte, racchiuso tra le pareti doppio in cipresso e il pavimento in tavole di cipresso produce un'acustica perfetta, amplificando le prestazioni dello strumento e rendendo lo spazio ideale per concerti intimi o per una riflessione personale sulla musica. La copertura del tetto è in pino giallo del sud, con una generosa spaziatura fra le travi; all'interno, la copertura ritrova il tradizionale azzurro dei portici dei ranch.

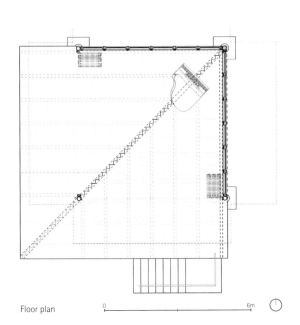

Floor plan

0   6m

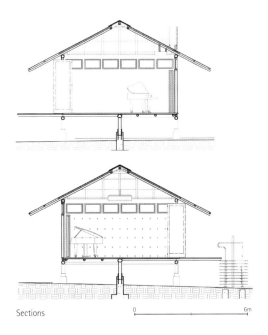

Sections

0   6m

Jordana Maisie has acquired a high level of expertise in the design and realisation of unusually imaginative projects. From gallery works to large-scale public art commissions, architectural and lighting design projects, the work has a profound commitment to user experience; creating innovative design-solutions with a dedication to artistic thinking and the latent potential of materials, craftsmanship and technology. Maisie has made work for Vogue, IBM and Feit. In 2014, she was invited to The White House to create an installation for The First Lady, Michelle Obama's Reach Higher initiative. After working for world-renowned studio Diller Scofidio + Renfro in NYC, Maisie made the move to LA where she is Creative Director of an interdisciplinary design studio focusing on an array of architectural, object and lighting design projects. With a background in photography, video production, sound engineering and interactive installation art, Maisie brings a fresh interdisciplinary approach to the art, architecture and design contexts.

JORDANA MAISIE
DESIGN STUDIO

WWW.JORDANAMAISIE.COM

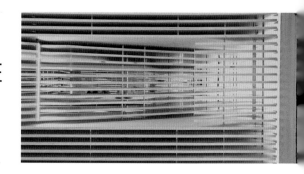

Jordana Maisie a acquis un niveau élevé de savoir-faire dans le design et la réalisation de projets de conception atypique. Ses travaux, de ses œuvres d'exposition à des commandes artistiques publiques, des projets de design architecturaux et d'éclairage à grande échelle, sont profondément engagés pour l'expérience de l'usager ; pour créer des solutions novatrices en s'attachant à la pensée artistique et au potentiel latent des matériaux, du savoir-faire artisanal et de la technologie. Maisie a travaillé pour Vogue, IBM et Feit. En 2014, elle a été invitée à la Maison Blanche pour créer une installation pour l'initiative Reach Higher de la Première Dame, Michelle Obama. Après avoir travaillé pour le studio à renommée mondiale Diller Scofidio + Renfro à New York, Maisie a déménagé à L.A. où elle est Directrice de création dans un studio de design qui se consacre à une variété de projets d'architecture et à la conception d'objets et d'éclairage. Avec son experience professionnelle, Maisie apporte une nouvelle approche interdisciplinaire aux contextes artistiques, architecturaux et de design.

Jordana Maisie è diventata una grande esperta di disegno e realizzazione di progetti particolarmente fantasiosi. Dalle opere da galleria fino agli incarichi di arte pubblica su vasta scala e ai progetti di design architettonico e dell'illuminazione, il suo lavoro è profondamente legato all'esperienza del cliente, e crea soluzioni innovative con un'attenzione speciale al pensiero artistico e al potenziale latente dei materiali, dell'artigianato e della tecnologia. Maisie ha lavorato per Vogue, IBM e Feit. Nel 2014 è stata invitata alla Casa Bianca per creare un'installazione appositamente per l'iniziativa Reach Higher della First Lady, Michelle Obama. Dopo aver lavorato per lo studio Diller Scofidio + Renfro di NYC, rinomato a livello mondiale, Maisie si è trasferita a LA, dove ricopre il ruolo di Direttrice Creativa in uno studio di design interdisciplinare incentrato su progetti di architettura, design di oggetti e illuminazione. Con la sua vasta esperienza professionale, Maisie adotta un fresco approccio interdisciplinare ai contesti artistici, architettonici e del design.

INSTALLATION ONE: RAW ELEMENTS OF CONSTRUCTION

INSTALLATION TWO: VOLUME AND VOID

The Installation prioritises FEIT's commitment to craftsmanship, every piece of furniture is a one off —nothing modular, each piece built onsite, entirely by hand, by two highly skilled carpenters. Cascading wooden planes emerge from the existing architecture into a split-level display showcasing the collection. The POS unit peels away from the adjacent wall, morphing into a functional work and display station. The incorporation of direct daylight into the design was also important; removing the awning to allow for direct morning light to activate the glazed display cabinet and reach deep into the store. The electrical lighting system was designed to define breaks in the program, separating display from service. A wall of vertically mounted fluorescent fixtures defines the boundary between retail display and areas dedicated to service (shoe repair and fitting areas). The integrated lighting and architectural design is key in playing with the user's perception of depth, producing a sense of wonder as users try to distinguish where the boundaries within the physical space lie.

INSTALLATION ONE:
RAW ELEMENTS OF CONSTRUCTION

© Naho Kubota, Ben Pogue

Cette installation priorise l'engagement de Feit envers le savoir-faire artisanal, chaque meuble étant unique – rien de modulaire, chaque pièce a été construite sur site, entièrement à la main, par deux menuisiers hautement qualifiés. Des pans de bois en cascade émergent des murs d'origine en un présentoir à deux niveaux pour exposer la collection. De même, le TPV se détache du mur adjacent, se transformant en poste de travail et d'exposition fonctionnel. L'incorporation de la lumière naturelle directe dans le design était également importante ; nous avons retiré le store pour permettre à la lumière du matin d'activer les vitrines et de pénétrer jusqu'au fond de la boutique. Le système d'éclairage électrique a été conçu pour définir des ruptures dans l'agencement, séparant étalage et service. Un mur d'aménagements fluorescents montés verticalement définit la frontière entre les zones de présentation pour la vente et les zones de service (cordonnerie et essayage). Pour jouer sur la perception de la profondeur chez les usagers, l'éclairage et le design architectural intégrés sont primordiaux, et produisent un sentiment d'étonnement lorsque ces derniers tentent de distinguer les limites de l'espace physique.

L'installazione si sviluppa secondo l'impegno di FEIT a privilegiare l'artigianato: ogni pezzo di arredamento è unico. Nessun elemento modulare: ogni pezzo è stato costruito in loco e interamente a mano, da due falegnami altamente qualificati. Piani di legno a cascata emergono dall'architettura preesistente e formano una vetrina su diversi livelli, dove disporre la collezione. L'unità POS si stacca dalla parete adiacente, per formare un'utile postazione di lavoro ed esposizione. Un ruolo molto importante nella progettazione è stato svolto anche dall'incorporazione della luce del giorno diretta. Abbiamo eliminato il tendone per permettere alla luce mattutina di accendere la vetrina e penetrare in tutto il negozio. Il sistema di illuminazione elettrica è stato progettato per sottolineare e separare l'area di esposizione da quella di servizio. Una parete di lampade fluorescenti montate in verticale definisce il confine tra l'esposizione per la vendita al dettaglio e la zona di servizio (riparazione e accessori). L'illuminazione integrata e il design architettonico sono fondamentali per la percezione della profondità, e producono un senso di meraviglia nel cliente che tenta di distinguere i confini dello spazio fisico.

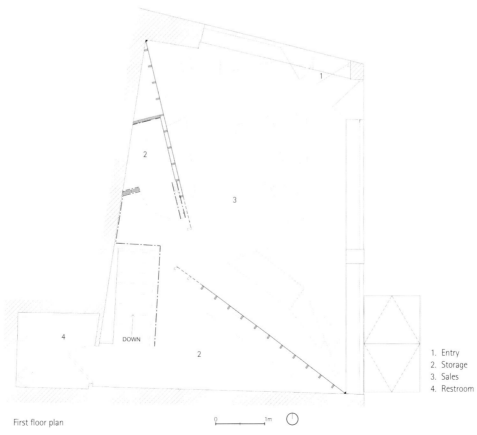

First floor plan

1. Entry
2. Storage
3. Sales
4. Restroom

0   1m

The Installation has a clean aesthetic featuring strong geometries created by volume and void. The design utilises a focused material palette, baltic birch plywood and stainless steel stand-offs, to create an immersive experience. Sheets of plywood are stacked to establish a sense of mass, and carved into to open up curated sight lines between different display areas within the space and back to the street. Similar to the process of moulding leather to a last, when 3D modeling the store, Maisie used volumetric moulds to carve out display areas within the slatted timber mass, the removal of the mould revealing the display space created. Each unique shape was CNC cut, hand sanded and assembled into modules offsite by the fabrication team, which enabled a complex build sequence to unroll on site. Mirror was used to open the space up and amplify the transparency of the birch ply installation. Both the architectural and lighting design play with your perception of depth. From an electric lighting perspective, the experience of the store differs by season as adjustable white LED's change in color temperature in accordance with summer, fall, winter, and spring.

INSTALLATION TWO: VOLUME AND VOID

© Naho Kubota, Nicholas Calcott

Cette installation a une esthétique épurée composée de géométries robustes créées par les volumes et les vides. Ce design utilise une palette de matériaux concentrée, contreplaqué de bouleau de la Baltique et séparateurs en inox, pour créer une expérience immersive. Des panneaux de contreplaqué sont superposés pour créer une impression de masse, et sculptés pour ouvrir des perspectives aménagées allant des différentes zones d'exposition vers l'intérieur de l'espace et jusque dans la rue. Dans un processus similaire à celui de la moulure de cuir sur un embauchoir, Maisie, en faisant un modèle 3D de la boutique, a utilisé des moules volumétriques pour creuser des zones d'étalage dans la masse de bois en lattes superposées, l'enlevage du moule révélant l'espace d'exposition ainsi créé. Chaque forme unique a été découpée à la machine CNC, sablée à la main et assemblée en modules hors-site par l'équipe de fabrication. Le miroir a été utilisé pour ouvrir l'espace et amplifier la transparence de l'installation. Le design architectural ainsi que celui de l'éclairage jouent sur notre perception de la profondeur. L'expérience de ce magasin diffère en fonction des saisons de par le changement de température de couleur des LED blanches selon qu'on est en été, en automne, en hiver ou en printemps.

L'installazione ha un'estetica pulita, caratterizzata da forti geometrie create dal gioco di volumi e vuoti. Il design utilizza una palette di materiali molto precisa: multistrato di betulla baltica ed elementi di collegamento in acciaio inox, per creare un'esperienza coinvolgente. I fogli in multistrato sono impilati per trasmettere una sensazione di massa. Le fessure tra un foglio e l'altro aprono lo sguardo su porzioni ben studiate delle diverse aree di esposizione all'interno dello spazio, e di nuovo verso la strada. Durante il processo di 3D modeling, Maisie ha usato modelli volumetrici per ricavare le zone di esposizione dalle doghe di legno, modelli che, una volta rimossi, hanno rivelato lo spazio espositivo realizzato. Ogni forma unica è stata fresata a CNC, sabbiata a mano e assemblata esternamente in moduli dalla squadra di costruzione. L'elemento a specchio ha contribuito ad ampliare lo spazio e valorizzare la trasparenza dell'installazione. Il design architettonico e quello dell'illuminazione giocano entrambi con la percezione della profondità. L'esperienza del negozio cambia a seconda della stagione. Un LED bianco regolabile, infatti, varia la temperatura del colore in funzione di estate, autunno, inverno e primavera.

Left mass. Views from above

Left mass. Views from below

Left mass. Views from above

Left mass. Views from below

Axonometric diagram of all parts

Knut Hjeltnes was born i Drøbak, Norway in 1961, and was raised in Ås, a small university town south of Oslo. He studied at the Norwegian Institute of Technology in Trondheim from 1980-86. During the latter half of his studies and for one and a half years after graduating he worked for 4B Architects. Since 1988 he has had his own practice. He taught at the Oslo school of Architecture from 1988-2016, the last 12 years as full professor. He has lectured in several countries, been awarded a number of prizes and his work is widely published.

The practice was established in Oslo as a one-man practice, slowly expanding to its current size of six employees. The office concentrates on homes, weekend houses and smaller public works. In a period over several years in the 1990s he cooperated with Haga and grov architects in Stavanger.

KNUT HJELTNES

WWW.HJELTNES.AS

Knut Hjeltnes est né à Drøbak, en Norvège, en 1961, et a grandi à Ås, petite ville universitaire au sud d'Oslo. Il a étudié à l'Institut de technologie de Trondheim de 1980 à 1986. Durant la deuxième partie de ses études et une année et demie après son diplôme il a travaillé pour 4B Architects. Depuis 1988 il a son propre cabinet. Il a enseigné à l'école d'architecture d'Oslo de 1988 à 2016, en tant que professeur à part entière les douze dernières années. Il a effectué des conférences dans plusieurs pays, a obtenu plusieurs prix et son travail fait l'objet de maintes publications.

Son cabinet, uniprofessionnel à l'origine, a été fondé à Oslo, s'agrandissant progressivement pour accueillir les six employés actuellement en fonction. Il se concentre sur les maisons, les habitations de week-end, et des travaux publics plus réduits. Sur une période de plusieurs années dans les années 1990 il a coopéré avec Haga & Grov architects à Stavanger.

Knut Hjeltnes è nato a Drøbak, Norvegia nel 1961, ed è cresciuto a Ås, cittadina universitaria a sud di Oslo. Ha studiato all'Università Norvegese della Scienza e della Tecnologia di Trondheim dal 1980 al 1986. Durante l'ultima metà degli studi e per un anno e mezzo dopo la laurea, ha lavorato per 4B Architects. Nel 1988 ha fondato il proprio studio. Ha insegnato alla Scuola di Oslo di Architettura e Design dal 1988 al 2016, gli ultimi 12 anni come docente ordinario. Ha tenuto conferenze in diversi paesi, vinto molti premi, e i suoi lavori sono pubblicati su scala internazionale.

Lo studio di Oslo, dapprima individuale, si è gradualmente ampliato fino ad accogliere gli attuali sei dipendenti. L'attività riguarda in prevalenza case, case per le vacanze e piccole opere pubbliche. Per gran parte degli anni '90 ha collaborato con gli architetti Haga & Grov a Stavanger.

WEEKEND HOUSE HANSEN/LINDSTAD
WEEKEND HOUSE STRAUME, SILDEGARNSHOLMEN

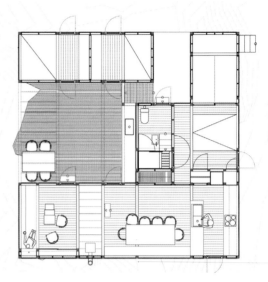

Main floor plan

The site of the summer house is located in Hvaler Archipelago, in south eastern Norway. No heavy machinery was used building the cabin and the very complex rock formation of the site is left completely intact. A precise topographical map was made enabling us to prefabricate the post and beam construction in glue laminated spruce. The construction is left visible on both in- and outside.

The placement of the cabin brigdes the lower part of the site with a natural plateau overlooking the sea below. Within the tight 10m x 10m square a complex spatial sequence evolves with rooms with varied ceiling heights and both sheltered and open outdoor spaces. Outside the walls are clad with fiber cement boards in different colours, in an irregular pattern. Inside walls and celings are aspen plywood.

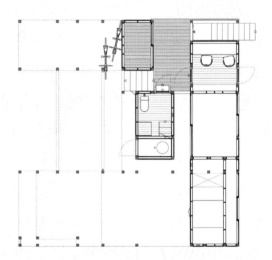

Basement plan

WEEKEND HOUSE HANSEN/LINDSTAD

© Sandra Aslaksen

Le site de cette maison d'été est situé dans l'archipel de Hvaler, au sud-est de la Norvège. Aucun engin lourd n'a été utilisé pour construire ce cabanon et la formation rocheuse très complexe du site a été laissée complètement intacte. Une carte topographique précise a été établie, nous permettant de pré-fabriquer la structure en poteaux et poutres d'épicéa lamellé-collé. Cette construction est laissée apparente à l'intérieur comme à l'extérieur.

L'emplacement de ce cabanon relie la partie inférieure du site avec un plateau naturel donnant sur la mer, en contrebas. Dans le carré de 10m sur 10m, une séquence spatiale complexe évolue avec des pièces aux hauteurs de plafonds variées et des espaces abrités ainsi qu'ouverts au plein air. À l'extérieur les murs sont bardés de panneaux de fibrociment de différentes couleurs, selon un schéma irrégulier. À l'intérieur, murs et plafonds sont en contreplaqué de tremble.

La casa per le vacanze estive si trova nell'Arcipelago di Hvaler, Norvegia sud-orientale. Nessun macchinario pesante è stato impiegato per costruire il cottage, e la complessa formazione rocciosa non è stata minimamente intaccata. Una dettagliata mappa topografica ci ha consentito di prefabbricare la struttura montanti e traversi in abete lamellare. Il materiale da costruzione è lasciato a vista sia all'interno che all'esterno.

Il cottage è posizionato in modo da collegare la parte inferiore del sito a un altopiano naturale che guarda sul mare. All'interno della stretta pianta di 10 x 10 m, si evolve una complessa sequenza spaziale, le stanze hanno soffitti di altezze diverse e sono presenti spazi chiusi e aperti. All'esterno, pannelli in fibro-cemento con forme diverse e trama irregolare rivestono i muri. Le pareti e i soffitti interni sono in compensato di pioppo.

An old timber warehouse was washed away by a hurricane in 1992 leaving only the stone foundation intact. We were allowed to erect a new building, with the same volume, reusing the old foundations. Because of the difficult building site it was decided to construct the complete 70 tons house on a nearby shipyard and lift it in place with an offshore crane. Seven steel frames establish the main construction, kept in place by the new concrete floor forming ground floor kitchen and living room. Four wooden volumes are mounted to these frames containing bathrooms, bedrooms and a media room. The attic is a large insulated storage space, also suited for parties or providing sleeping space for a fair number of guests.Sheltered outdoor areas between the outer timber envelope and the proper insulated facade are used for outside work, dining, relaxation and all kinds of odd storage needed for fishing and other outdoor activities.

WEEKEND HOUSE STRAUME, SILDEGARNSHOLMEN

© Handverksbygg, Inger Marie Grini, Knut Hjeltnes

Un vieil entrepôt en bois avait été emporté par un ouragan en 1992, ne laissant que les fondations, intactes. Nous avons été autorisés à ériger un nouveau bâtiment, aux mêmes volumes, en réutilisant les anciennes fondations. De par l'incommodité du site de construction il a été décidé de construire l'intégralité de la maison de 70 tonnes dans un chantier naval voisin et de le mettre en place par le biais d'une grue offshore. Sept cadres en acier établissent la construction principale, maintenue par le nouveau sol en béton formant la cuisine du rez-de-chaussée et le séjour. Quatre volumes en bois sont montés sur ces cadres contenant les salles-de-bain, les chambres et une salle multimédia. Les combles forment un espace de rangement spacieux et isolé qui peut également se prêter à des fêtes ou procurer du couchage pour un certain nombre d'invités. Les zones extérieures abritées entre l'enveloppe extérieure en bois et la façade isolée elle-même sont utilisées pour travailler dehors, dîner, se relaxer et pour toutes sortes de rangements nécessaires pour la pêche et autres activités de plein air.

Nel 1992, un uragano spazzò via un vecchio magazzino in legno, risparmiando solo le fondamenta di pietra. Su quelle vecchie fondamenta, siamo stati autorizzati a costruire un nuovo edificio dello stesso volume. A causa delle difficoltà presentate dall'area, abbiamo deciso di costruire l'intera casa da 70 t in un cantiere navale lì vicino, e trasferirla poi sul posto con una gru offshore. Sette strutture in acciaio, tenute insieme dal nuovo pavimento di cemento che forma la cucina e il soggiorno del piano terra, costituiscono l'elemento principale della costruzione. Su queste, sono montati quattro volumi in legno, contenenti i bagni, le camere da letto e una sala multimediale. L'attico è un grande spazio/deposito coibentato, adatto anche per le feste o per fungere da camera da letto per un discreto numero di ospiti. Le aree esterne coperte, tra l'involucro in legno e la vera facciata isolata, vengono utilizzate per lavorare all'aperto, mangiare, rilassarsi e per tutte le particolari esigenze di deposito create dalla pesca e da altre attività all'aperto.

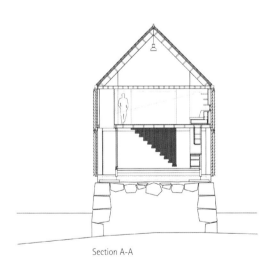

Section A-A

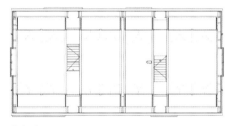

Attic plan

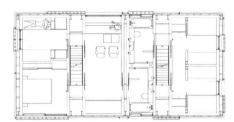

First floor plan

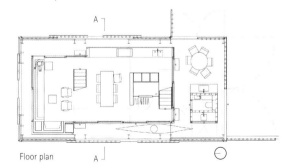

Floor plan

A

A

With our multidisciplinary team, we have been implementing ambitious building and interior design projects since 1994. We work in an informal, professional atmosphere, which is characterised by our passion for the job, both within the office and in our dealings with our clients. Top-class projects can result only from reliable partnership relations. Premium quality is shown on the one hand by pioneering architecture, and on the other by the appreciation of beauty and tradition. In the course of time, we have developed a sense of quality that is based on sustainable, durable materials and efficient technologies. At the same time, we design classical and modern buildings and spatial concepts. In this sense, our projects can look back over a wonderful history while being completely up-to-date.

LANDAU + KINDELBACHER
ARCHITEKTEN-INNENARCHITEKTEN

WWW.LANDAUKINDELBACHER.DE

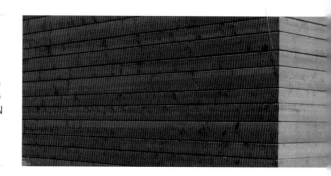

Depuis 1994, notre équipe multidisciplinaire met en œuvre d'ambitieux projets de construction et d'architecture d'intérieur. Nous travaillons dans une atmosphère informelle, professionnelle, qui se caractérise par notre passion pour ce travail, au bureau comme dans nos interactions avec nos clients. Les projets de haut niveau ne peuvent naître que de relations de partenariat fiables. Une qualité supérieure se révèle d'une part dans une architecture novatrice, et de l'autre dans l'appréciation de la beauté et de la tradition. Au fil du temps, nous avons développé une notion de qualité qui s'appuie sur des matériaux durables, résistants et des technologies efficaces. En même temps, nous concevons des bâtiments classiques et modernes et des concepts d'espace. En ce sens, nos projets peuvent renvoyer à une Histoire fabuleuse tout en étant complètement actuels.

Realizziamo ambiziosi progetti di edifici e design di interni sin dal 1994, insieme al nostro team multidisciplinare. Lavoriamo in un'atmosfera informale e professionale, caratterizzata dalla passione per il nostro mestiere, sia all'interno dell'ufficio che nelle trattative con i nostri clienti. Progetti di prim'ordine possono essere figli solo di partnership affidabili. L'architettura pionieristica da un lato e la rivalutazione della bellezza e della tradizione dall'altro evidenziano la qualità superiore. Nel tempo, abbiamo sviluppato un senso della qualità che poggia su materiali sostenibili e durevoli, oltre che su tecnologie efficienti. Al contempo, progettiamo edifici classici, moderni e soluzioni spaziali. In questo senso, i nostri progetti guardano all'eccezionale storia del passato rimanendo interamente attuali.

HOUSE BY THE LAKE

Building plots with lake access in Munich's "Fünfseenland" (Five Lakes Region) are rare. All the luckier for the owners of this house with its fantastic location and the panoramic view of the Bavarian Alpine foreland. The site is characterised by its location on a steep slope with mature woodland, so that the entrance at street level leads to a two-storey living space stretching into the roof. Instead of a single large building, the rooms of the house with the adjacent building are distributed across two separate volumes, which develop as simple, compact structures. The archetypal construction absorbs the local form language, aptly translated in materiality and space usage requirements. The solid natural stone plinth made of Wachenzell dolomite appears to grow out of the slope, whereas the rear-ventilated timber façade of rough-sawn spruce symbolises the attachment to the surroundings but through its form and colourfulness is the result of a completely modern interpretation. Towards the road, the façade is closed, but towards the lake is much more open.

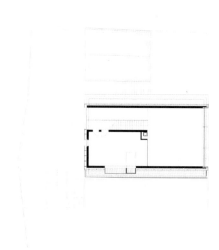

Upper main floor plan

HOUSE BY THE LAKE

© Christian Hacker

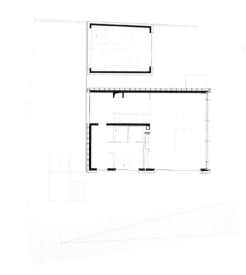

Intermediate floor plan

Les parcelles bénéficiant d'un accès au lac dans la région des « Fünfseenland » (cinq lacs) de Munich sont rares. Les propriétaires de cette maison à l'emplacement fantastique et aux vues panoramiques sur l'avant-pays alpin bavarois n'en sont que plus chanceux. Ce site se caractérise par son emplacement sur une côte abrupte de forêts anciennes, de sorte que l'entrée au niveau de la rue mène à un espace à vivre de deux étages qui s'étend jusque sous la toiture. Au lieu de former un seul grand espace, les pièces de cette habitation avec un bâtiment adjacent sont distribuées dans deux volumes séparés, ce qui donne des structures simples et compactes. Cette construction archétypique intègre le langage local des formes, judicieusement traduit dans les besoins en matière de matérialité et d'usage de l'espace. Le soubassement de pierre naturelle massive en dolomite *Wachenzell* semble sortir de la colline, tandis que la façade bardée d'épicéa brut de sciage, à ventilation arrière, symbolise l'attachement à l'environnement mais, par sa forme et son aspect coloré, est le résultat d'une interprétation résolument moderne. Du côté de la route, la façade est fermée, mais du côté du lac elle est bien plus ouverte.

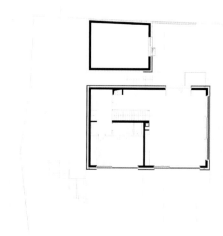

Nella regione dei cinque laghi (Fünfseenland), vicino Monaco di Baviera, le aree edificabili con accesso al lago sono rare. Circostanza più che fortunata per i proprietari di questa casa, con la sua posizione fantastica e il panorama mozzafiato sulla zona prealpina bavarese. La particolarità del sito sta nella posizione su un ripido pendio con ambienti di bosco maturo, cosicché l'ingresso al livello della strada conduce a uno spazio abitativo su due piani che si estende nel tetto. Invece di una grande costruzione singola, le stanze della casa con l'edificio adiacente sono distribuite su due volumi separati sviluppantisi come strutture semplici e compatte. La costruzione originale assorbe il linguaggio delle forme locali, adeguatamente tradotto in materialità ed esigenze di uso dello spazio. Lo zoccolo di solida pietra naturale in dolomite di Wachenzell sembra nascere dal pendio, mentre la facciata ventilata in legno di abete dal taglio grezzo simboleggia l'attaccamento all'ambiente circostante, risultandone però interpretazione del tutto moderna grazie a forma e varietà di colori. La facciata è chiusa verso la strada, preferendo aprirsi molto di più davanti al lago.

Ground floor plan

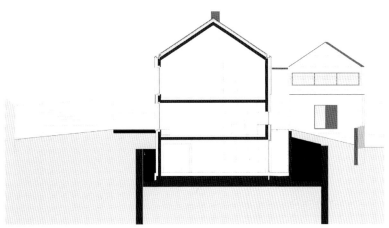

Section

Lukkaroinen Architects was established by Pekka Lukkaroinen in 1980 in Oulu, northern Finland. Its first one-man office was situated in a cellar of a block of flats. In the beginning the company focused mainly on land-use planning for nearby municipalities. Building design soon took its place as the Lukkaroinen Architects' main sector. So far the company has designed schools, hospitals and commercial buildings from the very south of Finland to north of the Arctic Circle. Nowadays Lukkaroinen Architects is one of the leading designers of schools and hospitals in the country. In the 2010s, the company stregthened its foothold in the Helsinki metropolitan area by establishing an office in the capital. Over the years, Lukkaroinen Architects has grown from one-man office to a company of nearly 60 employees. In 2016, Lukkaroinen acquired its long-term collaboration partner, the highly-regarded interior design firm Ervasti, thereby adding interior design into its service portfolio.

LUKKAROINEN ARCHITECTS

WWW.LUKKAROINEN.FI

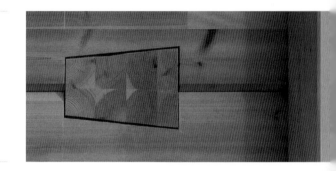

Lukkaroinen Architects a été fondé par Pekka Lukkaroinen en 1980 à Oulu, au Nord de la Finlande. Son premier cabinet était situé dans la cave d'un immeuble. Au début cette société se concentrait essentiellement sur les plans locaux d'occupation des terres pour des municipalités locales. Le design de bâtiments est rapidement devenu le secteur principal de Lukkaroinen Architects. Depuis cette société a conçu des écoles, des hôpitaux et des bâtiments commerciaux de la pointe Sud de la Finlande au Nord du Cercle polaire. Aujourd'hui elle est l'un des principaux concepteurs d'écoles et d'hôpitaux du pays. Dans les années 2010, Lukkaroinen Architects a renforcé sa présence dans la région métropolitaine d'Helsinki en créant une étude dans la capitale. Au fil des années, elle est passée de cabinet uniprofessionnel à une société de presque 60 employés. En 2016, Lukkaroinen s'est acquis la société d'architecture d'intérieur très prisée Ervasti, son collaborateur de toujours, ajoutant ainsi le design d'intérieur à son portfolio de services.

Lukkaroinen Architects è stato fondato nel 1980 da Pekka Lukkaroinen a Oulu, nella Finlandia settentrionale. La prima sede individuale era situata nella cantina di un condominio. Agli esordi, lo studio si concentra principalmente sulla pianificazione territoriale dei comuni limitrofi. Presto, però, la progettazione di edifici diventa il settore di punta di Lukkaroinen Architects. Lo studio ha progettato scuole, ospedali ed edifici commerciali dalle zone più meridionali della Finlandia fino alla parte settentrionale del Circolo Polare Artico. Oggi, Lukkaroinen Architects è uno dei più importanti progettisti di scuole e ospedali del paese. Negli anni 2010, lo studio ha conquistato una posizione sicura nell'area metropolitana di Helsinki aprendo una sede nella capitale. Nel corso degli anni, Lukkaroinen Architects si è evoluto da studio individuale ad azienda con circa 60 dipendenti. Nel 2016, Lukkaroinen si è unito al rinomato studio di interior design Ervasti in una partnership duratura, aggiungendo quindi il design di interni alla sua gamma di servizi.

PUDASJÄRVI LOG CAMPUS

Pudasjärvi Log Campus comprehends primary school, secondary school and upper secondary school. Wooden structures and components are used comprehensively in the whole building. The structural walls are made of laminated log with few exceptions due to building code. The exterior log walls of 275 mm provide insulation against varying temperatures. The roofs of the main hall and lanterns are supported by glulam pillars and beams with various shapes. Cross-laminated timber elements are used in the floors and the CNC cut banisters of the main hall stairways. The color palette is a dialogue between tranquil natural wood shades and vivid details. The indoor log surfaces are protected by transparent wax coating maintaining the natural character of wood, and joyful colors in the boards of the fixtures and panels covering the settling gaps (detail distinctive for log structures) invigorate the space. Similarly, in the outside facades the color palette of the log surfaces is down-to-earth compared to the bright board cladding.

PUDASJÄRVI LOG CAMPUS

© RA-Studio Raimo Ahonen

Pudasjärvi Log Campus comprend école primaire, école secondaire et lycée. Structures et éléments en bois y sont amplement utilisés dans tout le bâtiment. Les murs porteurs sont composés de madriers contrecollés à quelques exceptions près, en raison du code du bâtiment. Les murs extérieurs de 275 mm composés de madriers empilés procurent une isolation contre les variations de températures. Les toits de l'entrée principale et les lanternes sont soutenus par des piliers et des poutres de lamellé-collé aux formes diverses. Les éléments en bois contrecollé sont utilisés pour les sols et les rampes découpées au laser des escaliers de l'entrée principale. La palette de couleurs est un dialogue entre les teintes apaisées du bois naturel et les détails bariolés. Les surfaces intérieures en rondins sont protégées par une couche de cire transparente qui conserve l'aspect naturel du bois, et des couleurs chatoyantes sur les planches des aménagements et des panneaux couvrant les joints de dilatation (un détail distinctif pour les structures en bois empilé) dynamisent l'espace. De même, dans les façades extérieures, la palette des surfaces de bois est terne comparée au bardage aux couleurs vives.

Il Log campus di Pudasjärvi comprende scuola primaria, secondaria e secondaria superiore. L'intera costruzione ha previsto l'uso esteso di strutture e componenti in legno. I muri portanti sono composti da travi laminate, con poche eccezioni dovute al codice edilizio. I muri esterni da 275 mm, composti anch'essi da travi, proteggono dalle variazioni della temperatura. Le coperture dell'atrio principale e le lampade sono sostenute da pilastri e travi in legno lamellare incollato di forme diverse. Per i pavimenti e le ringhiere delle scale nell'atrio principale, ottenute con taglio CNC, sono stati scelti elementi in legno laminato incrociato. La tavolozza è un dialogo tra la tranquillità del legno naturale e la vividezza dei dettagli. Le superfici interne e le travi che le compongono sono protette da un rivestimento in cera trasparente, che mantiene il colore naturale del legno. I colori allegri scelti per le installazioni e i pannelli che coprono le fessure (dettaglio tipico delle strutture in tronchi) animano lo spazio. Allo stesso modo, sulle facciate esterne, le superfici dei tronchi hanno una gamma di colore dai toni semplici, se paragonata a quelli brillanti del rivestimento di assi.

Second floor plan

1. Cookery
2. Science classrooms
3. Student welfare
4. Administration

0   25m

First floor plan

1. Main entrance
2. Service
3. Carpentry & metal work
4. Kitchen
5. Canteen
6. Sports & events
7. Music & visual arts
8. Primary school
9. Secondary school
10. Schoolyard

0   25m

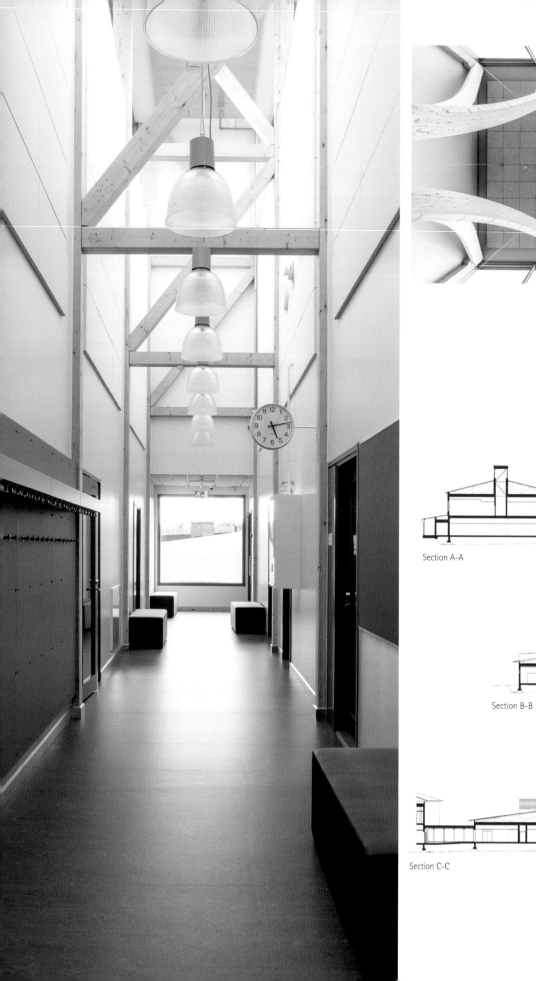

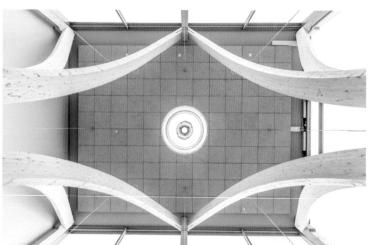

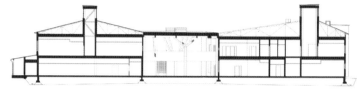

Section A-A

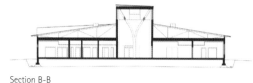

Section B-B

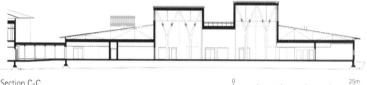

Section C-C

0   25m

Lund Hagem is an architecture and urban design practice based in Oslo. The office was founded in 1990, and today it is managed by five partners; Svein Lund, Einar Hagem, Mette Røsbekk, Per Suul and Kristine Strøm-Gundersen. All projects are informed by a sensitive approach to the surrounding landscape and a dynamic dialogue between nature and the built environment. The work of Lund Hagem focuses on critical detailing and economic of means both poetically and practically.

Our designs reflect our belief in combining the latest advances in building technology with sustainable techniques and materiality drawn from local tradition. This provides us with key knowledge and experience in designing energy efficient Passive Houses and sustainable BREEAM certified buildings. We have in-office certification BREEAM Accredited Professional (BREEAM AP). Lund Hagem is a member of Norwegian Green Building Council.

© Dennis Alekseev, Lund Hagem

LUND HAGEM
ARKITEKTER

WWW.LUNDHAGEM.NO

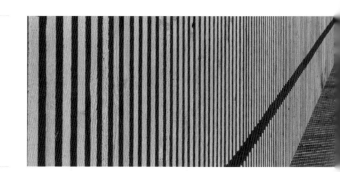

Lund Hagem est un cabinet d'architecture et d'urbanisme basé à Oslo. Ce bureau a été fondé en 1990, et il est aujourd'hui géré par cinq partenaires : Svein Lund, Einar Hagem, Mette Røsbekk, Per Suul et Kristine Strøm-Gundersen. Tous les projets sont nourris par un rapport sensible au paysage environnant et par un dialogue entre la nature et l'environnement bâti. Les travaux de Lund Hagem se concentrent sur les détails primordiaux d'exécution et sur l'économie de moyens au point de vue à la fois poétique et pratique. Nos designs reflètent notre foi dans l'alliance entre les derniers progrès de la technologie du bâtiment et les techniques durables et la matérialité tirées de la tradition locale. Cela nous procure des connaissances et une expérience primordiales dans la conception de maisons passives et de constructions certifiées BREEAM à haute efficacité énergétique. Nous comptons parmi nous un professionnel accrédité BREEAM (BREEAM AP). Lund Hagem est membre du Conseil norvégien de l'habitat écologique (Norwegian Green Building Council).

Lund Hagem è uno studio di architettura e urban design con sede a Oslo. Fondato nel 1990, è oggi gestito da cinque partner: Svein Lund, Einar Hagem, Mette Røsbekk, Per Suul e Kristine Strøm-Gundersen. Tutti i progetti sono guidati da un approccio empatico all'ambiente circostante, e da un dialogo dinamico tra la natura e il paesaggio urbano. I lavori di Lund Hagem si concentrano sull'importanza dei dettagli e l'economia di mezzi, sia in senso poetico che pratico. I nostri progetti riflettono ciò in cui crediamo: l'unione tra i più recenti progressi della tecnologia edilizia e le tecniche sostenibili ereditate dalla tradizione locale, scelta dei materiali compresa. È così che acquisiamo conoscenza ed esperienza nella progettazione di Case Passive efficienti dal punto di vista energetico ed edifici sostenibili certificati BREEAM. Abbiamo al nostro interno un BREEAM AP, figura professionale formata e certificata da BREEAM. Lund Hagem è un membro del Norwegian Green Building Council.

CABIN KVITFJELL

LILLE ARØYA

The site is located at one of the highest buildable plots within the Kvitfjell Ski Resort hosting uninterrupted views and dramatic topography. The vegetation consisting of birch and pine trees create a natural filter towards the road, and the ski resort further down the mountain. The two volumes are placed near the site boarders, thus creating a sheltered "courtyard" open to the evening sun. The main cabin and the annex are built on stilts, not to interfere with the ground. To emphasise the idea of the summer cabin in the mountain, the volumes are wrapped in thin, vertical louvers. Creating a light "veil-like" quality towards the courtyard as well as protecting the recessed glass behind. The plan is shaped to frame the remarkable views over the mountains, from both the common areas and the master bedroom. Ore-pine louvers treated with iron sulphate cover the exterior layer whereas painted Pine covers the inner exterior and interior facades. The outside floors and ceilings are untreated Pine, the inside is oiled Oak.

CABIN KVITFJELL

© Sam Hughes, Marc Goodwin

Ce site se trouve sur l'une des parcelles constructibles les plus élevées de la station de ski Kvitfjell, avec des vues dégagées et une topographie saisissante. La végétation composée de bouleaux et de pins crée un filtre naturel en bordure de route, et vers la station plus loin dans la montagne. Ces deux volumes sont placés près des frontières du site, créant ainsi une « cour » abritée ouverte au soleil du soir. La cabane principale et l'annexe sont construites sur pilotis, pour éviter toute interférence avec le sol. Pour accentuer le concept de la cabane d'été dans la montagne, les volumes sont enveloppés dans de fines persiennes verticales, créant une qualité légèrement « voilée » du côté de la cour tout en protégeant le renfoncement vitré situé derrière. La forme du plan est conçue pour encadrer les vues remarquables au-dessus des montagnes, depuis les zones communes ainsi que la chambre principale. Les persiennes de pin durci traité au sulfate de fer recouvrent l'enveloppe extérieure tandis que des lames peintes enveloppent les façades internes à l'intérieur et à l'extérieur. Les sols et plafonds sont en pin non-traité, l'intérieur en chêne huilé.

Il posto è situato in una delle aree edificabili più elevate all'interno del Kvitfjell Ski Resort, con i loro panorami ininterrotti e la spettacolare topografia. La vegetazione formata da betulle e pini crea una protezione naturale dalla strada e dalla stazione sciistica situata più in basso. I due volumi sono collocati vicino ai confini dell'area, in moda da creare una "corte" protetta, ma aperta al sole della sera. La baita principale e la sua dependance sono costruite su palafitte, per non interferire con il terreno. Per esaltare l'idea della baita estiva, i volumi sono avvolti da sottili persiane verticali. L'effetto è quello di un leggero "velo" che si stende sulla corte, mentre dal punto di vista pratico si ha una protezione delle finestre incassate sottostanti. Il progetto è concepito per incorniciare i magnifici panorami sulle montagne, sia dalle zone comuni che dalla camera da letto padronale. Le persiane in pino minerale e trattate con solfato ferroso ricoprono le pareti esterne, mentre all'interno le facciate esterne e interne sono rivestite in legno di pino. Pavimenti e soffitti esterni sono in pino non trattato, quelli interni in legno di quercia oliato.

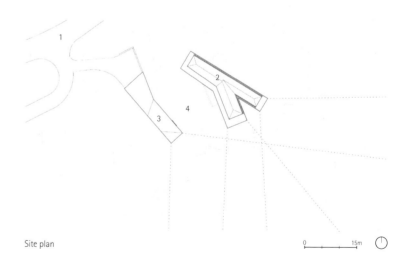

Site plan

0   15m

1. Road
2. Main cabin
3. Carport / Annex
4. Courtyard

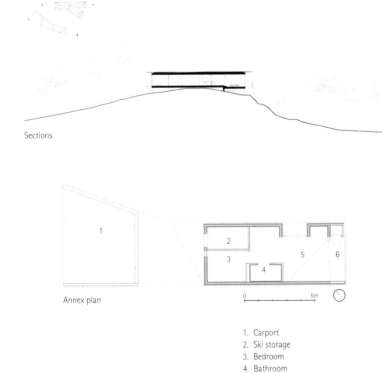

Sections

Annex plan

0   5m

1. Carport
2. Ski storage
3. Bedroom
4. Bathroom
5. Living room
6. Balcony

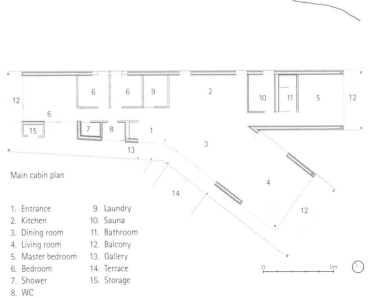

Main cabin plan

0   5m

1. Entrance
2. Kitchen
3. Dining room
4. Living room
5. Master bedroom
6. Bedroom
7. Shower
8. WC
9. Laundry
10. Sauna
11. Bathroom
12. Balcony
13. Gallery
14. Terrace
15. Storage

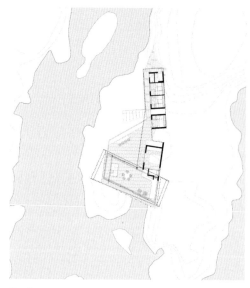

Site plan

The site consists of a series of small island connected by hand-built bridges making a continuous and inhabitable landscape. The lack of flat surfaces, the closeness to the water and the desire not to interfere with the rock, dictated a solution out of the ordinary. The building creates a site on stilts that latches onto the island to unite the new with the old. Bedrooms and bathrooms are located in volumes placed on the threshold between the island and the new surface, whereas the roof spanning across the new deck creates a shelter for living.

The timber structure is visible forming the exterior and the interior. Glulam beams span from inside to outside and together with raw steel columns and a white concrete fireplace shape and colour the interior. Solid steel columns carry the "new site" for the house. The materials are kept to a minimum. Ore Pine is used outside and inside. Some of the exterior is stained black to tie in with the surroundings, the rest is left to patinate.

LILLE ARØYA

© Alexander Westberg, Ivar Kvaal, Lund Hagem

Ce site est composé d'une série de petites îles reliées entre elles par des ponts construits de façon artisanale, ce qui crée un paysage continu et hospitalier. L'absence de surfaces planes, la proximité de l'eau et le désir de ne pas interférer avec la roche ont inspiré une solution hors du commun. Ce bâtiment crée un site sur pilotis qui s'accroche à l'île pour réunir l'ancien et le nouveau. Les chambres et salles-de-bain sont situées dans des volumes implantés sur le seuil entre l'île et la nouvelle surface, tandis que le toit qui s'étend sur la nouvelle terrasse crée un abri à vivre.

La structure en bois est visible, formant l'extérieur et l'intérieur. Les poutres en lamellé-collé filent de l'intérieur vers l'extérieur et, alliées à des colonnes d'acier brut et à un âtre en béton blanc, façonnent et colorent l'intérieur. Des colonnes d'acier massif soutiennent le « nouveau site » de la maison. Le nombre de matériaux est restreint. Le pin durci est utilisé pour l'extérieur comme l'intérieur. À l'extérieur il est parfois teint en noir pour se fondre dans son environnement, le reste étant destiné à être patiné par le temps.

L'area è formata da una serie di isolotti collegati tra loro da ponti rudimentali che ne fanno un paesaggio ininterrotto e abitabile. La mancanza di superfici piatte, la vicinanza all'acqua e il desiderio di non interferire con la roccia hanno suggerito una soluzione fuori dall'ordinario. L'edificio crea un'area su palafitte che si aggancia all'isola per riunire il nuovo con l'ancestrale. Le camere da letto e i bagni sono posizionati all'interno di volumi posti sulla soglia tra l'isola e la nuova superficie, mentre il tetto che si estende sul tutto il ponte di nuova costruzione fa di questo un posto riparato da vivere.

La struttura in legno compone visibilmente la parte esterna e quella interna. Il legno lamellare incollato si fa strada dall'interno verso l'esterno, e insieme alle colonne in acciaio grezzo e al caminetto in calcestruzzo bianco dà forma e colora gli ambienti coperti. Sono le colonne in acciaio massiccio a determinare il "nuovo" della casa. I materiali sono ridotti al minimo. All'esterno come all'interno, pino minerale. Alcune parti esterne sono macchiate di nero per richiamare l'ambiente circostante, il resto è lasciato all'azione degli elementi.

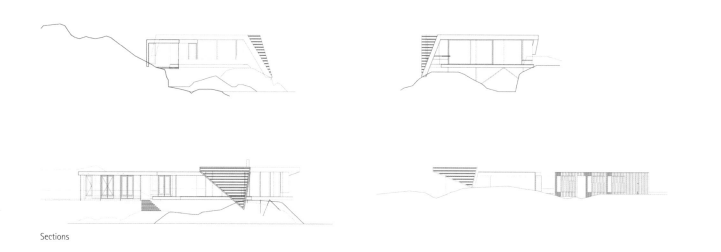

Sections

Marlene Uldschmidt studied architecture at HAWK University of Applied Sciences and Arts, Faculty of Architecture, Engineering and Conservation. For several years she specialized in conservation projects in Germany. MARLENE ULDSCHMIDT ARCHITECTS was founded in Ferragudo Algarve in 2005. Marlene is a member of Architektenkammer Germany, Association of Architects Portugal, Royal Institute of British Architects RIBA.

The studio believes that architecture and design should be in context with the habitat, topography and heritage of the location of the site. A balance between architecture, landscape and people is central to each project. Our imaginative concepts combine natural materials and contemporary design to create volumes of light and space. The use of local craftsmen and materials are also an integral part of the design journey.

MARLENE ULDSCHMIDT

WWW.MARLENEULDSCHMIDT.COM

Marlene Uldschmidt a étudié l'architecture à la Faculté d'architecture, d'ingénierie et de conservation de la *HAWK University of Applied Sciences and Arts*. Pendant plusieurs années elle s'est spécialisée dans des projets de conservation en Allemagne. MARLENE ULDSCHMIDT ARCHITECTS a été fondé à Ferragudo, en Algarve, en 2005. Marlene est membre de *Architektenkammer Germany*, de l'ordre des architectes du Portugal, du *Royal Institute of British Architects* RIBA.

Le credo de ce studio est que l'architecture et le design devraient être contextualisés dans l'habitat, la topographie et le patrimoine de l'emplacement d'un site. Un équilibre entre architecture, paysage et personnes est au centre de chaque projet. Nos concepts imaginatifs associent matériaux naturels et design contemporain pour créer des volumes de lumière et d'espace. L'utilisation d'artisans et de matériaux locaux fait partie intégrante du processus de conception.

Marlene Uldschmidt ha studiato architettura alla HAWK, Università di scienze applicate e arti, Facoltà di Architettura, Ingegneria e Conservazione. Per molti anni ha lavorato in Germania, specializzandosi in progetti di conservazione. Ha fondato lo studio MARLENE ULDSCHMIDT ARCHITECTS nel 2005 a Ferragudo, nell'Algarve. Marlene è membro della Architektenkammer tedesca, dell'Associazione portoghese degli architetti, e del Royal Institute of British Architects RIBA.

Lo studio crede che architettura e design debbano essere coerenti con l'habitat, la topografia e l'eredità del luogo. Fondamentale per il progetto, l'equilibrio tra architettura, paesaggio e persone. Il nostro concetto di creatività mette insieme materiali naturali e design contemporaneo per creare volumi di luce e spazio. Coinvolgere gli artigiani e utilizzare i materiali del posto sono anch'essi aspetti integranti del nostro viaggio nella progettazione.

THE PAVILLION

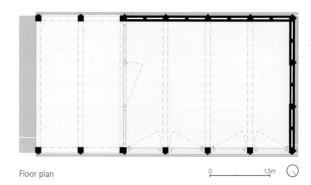

Floor plan   0   1,5m

The Pavillion has been designed as a modern day folly, is constructed of timber and glass and is located in the grounds of an existing detached villa in the Algarve.

The concept was to create a small private retreat close to the existing house with views across open countryside towards the sea beyond. The new structure is sited in a wonderfully mature setting but also in a part of the garden that was rarely used. Subtle changes are projected onto the timber slatted façade throughout the day created by the movement of the sun and the shadows from the foliage of the surrounding trees. A dramatic change occurs in its appearance when lit at night. The main secret of the building, the glorious south facing vista, can only be viewed from inside the contemporary installation.

THE PAVILLION

© Fernando Guerra | FG+SG

Le Pavillon a été conçu comme une fabrique de jardin des temps modernes, construit en bois et verre et situé sur le terrain d'une villa individuelle de l'Algarve.

Le concept consistait à créer un petit refuge près de la maison principale avec des vues sur une campagne dégagée jusqu'à la mer à l'horizon. Cette nouvelle structure est implantée dans un cadre merveilleusement épanoui, qui est aussi une partie du jardin qui était rarement utilisée. Des changements subtils sont projetés sur la façade de lattes de bois tout au long de la journée, créés par le mouvement du soleil et des ombres du feuillage des arbres environnants. Une véritable métamorphose s'opère dans son apparence lorsqu'il est allumé la nuit. Le secret principal de cette construction, sa magnifique vue sur le sud, ne peut être découvert que par l'intérieur de cette installation contemporaine.

The Pavillion è stato progettato come una follia del nostri giorni; costruito in legno e vetro, si trova nel parco di una preesistente villa bifamiliare nell'Algarve.

L'idea era di costruire un piccolo ritiro privato nei pressi della casa, con vista sull'aperta campagna che si estende fino al mare. La nuova struttura è ubicata in un meraviglioso ambiente verde, ma anche in una parte del giardino il cui utilizzo era sporadico. Il movimento del sole e le ombre create dalle foglie proiettano durante il giorno delicate variazioni sulla facciata a doghe. Se illuminata al buio, la struttura mostra un cambiamento radicale. Il principale segreto dell'edificio, il magnifico panorama verso sud, si svela soltanto dall'interno di questa installazione contemporanea.

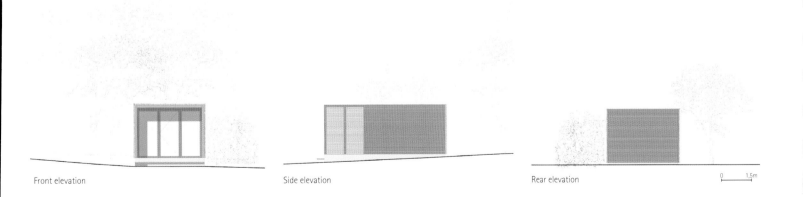

Front elevation

Side elevation

Rear elevation

0   1,5m

Maryann Thompson Architects (MTA) is a Cambridge-based architecture firm that offers a wide range of services to public and private clients. We specialize in architecture that is sustainable, regionally driven and that attempts to heighten the phenomenological qualities of the site in which we work. Architectural investigations revolve around such concerns as the creation of a rich and thoughtful edge between inside and outside, utilizing light as a medium, and employing warm, natural materials in order to accentuate a sense of place. The firm's staff comes from diverse backgrounds, including architecture, landscape architecture, green architecture, planning, interior design, and the visual arts. MTA includes LEED Accredited professionals, and Maryann carries degrees in both architecture and landscape architecture, bringing to the practice an interdisciplinary approach where issues of the landscape and the environment are central to our design thinking.

MARYANN THOMPSON ARCHITECTS

WWW.MARYANNTHOMPSON.COM

Maryann Thompson Architects (MTA) est un bureau d'architecture basé à Cambridge qui offre une variété de services à une clientèle publique et privée. Nous sommes spécialisés dans une architecture durable, axée sur le local et qui cherche à accentuer les qualités phénoménologiques du site sur lequel nous travaillons. Nos recherches architecturales sont centrées sur des préoccupations telles que la création d'une zone riche et raisonnée entre l'intérieur et l'extérieur, usant de la lumière comme médium, et employant des matériaux chaleureux, naturels pour accentuer le sentiment d'appartenance au lieu. Les employés du cabinet proviennent de divers univers, comme l'architecture, le paysagisme, l'architecture, la planification, l'architecture intérieure écologiques, et les arts visuels. MATA comprend des professionnels accrédités LEED, et Maryann est titulaire de diplômes en architecture et en architecture paysager, ce qui apporte à sa pratique une approche interdisciplinaire dans laquelle les questions de paysage et d'environnement sont au cœur de la pensée conceptrice.

Maryann Thompson Architects (MTA) è uno studio di architettura con sede a Cambridge, che offre una grande varietà di servizi a clienti pubblici e privati. Siamo specializzati in architettura sostenibile, orientata al territorio e che si impegna a elevare le qualità fenomenologiche dell'area in cui operiamo. Le indagini architettoniche si muovono attorno a questioni come la creazione di un confine ricco e attento tra interno ed esterno, che utilizzi la luce come un mezzo e materiali caldi e naturali per accentuare il senso del luogo. Lo staff dello studio viene da background diversi, che includono l'architettura, l'architettura del paesaggio, l'architettura verde, la pianificazione, l'interior design e le arti visive. MTA comprende professionisti accreditati LEED, e Maryann è laureata in architettura e architettura del paesaggio. Questa formazione fa sì che lo studio abbia un approccio interdisciplinare che mette in primo piano nel design thinking le questioni legate al territorio e all'ambiente.

THE OAKS

This house, within an ancient oak grove, wraps an existing hilltop knoll, rather than sitting atop it. This siting strategy allows for the primary reading and figure of the project, upon approach, to be that of the ferns, trees and sloped ground of the site. The interior of the house develops along and unfolding spatial sequence that constantly orients and reorients the viewer to the site as one moves through the project, knitting the site and the house together. The main living area of the house is oriented to the low sculptural branches of the large oaks at the top of the hill, angled to the south for sunlight. Overhangs and trellises shield the summer sun, yet are sized to let in winter light. The light shelf, under the clerestory, is glazed with reflective glass and throws a line of light onto the ceiling, dappled with the play of leaves in its reflection, bringing the patterns of the site deep into the project. The house also responds to the site in its material palate.

THE OAKS

© Chuck Choi Architectural Photography

Cette maison, implantée dans une ancienne chênaie, couronne la calotte d'un tertre existant, plutôt que d'être installée à son sommet. Cette stratégie d'implantation permet à la lecture et à la figuration principales de ce projet d'être celles des fougères, des arbres et du terrain en pente du site. L'intérieur de la maison se développe au fil de cette séquence spatiale qui oriente et réoriente constamment l'observateur vers le site tandis que celui-ci traverse le projet, associant le site avec la maison. La pièce à vivre principale est tournée vers les branches basses sculpturales des grands chênes au sommet de la colline, orientée vers le sud pour la lumière. Des avancées et des treillages protègent du soleil d'été, mais sont dimensionnés de façon à laisser passer la lumière en hiver. L'étagère légère, sous les claires-voies, est en miroir réfléchissant et renvoie un faisceau de lumière vers le plafond, pommelé par le jeu des feuilles dans son reflet, apportant les motifs du site au cœur du projet. Cette maison est également liée à son implantation de par sa palette de matériaux.

La dimora, integrata in un antico bosco di querce, piuttosto che appollaiarsi sulla cima di una collinetta esistente, si sviluppa attorno a essa. Questa strategia di collocazione consente alla lettura e alla cifra principali del progetto di realizzarsi nelle felci, negli alberi e nel terreno irregolare dell'area. L'interno della casa si sviluppa svelando una sequenza dello spazio che orienta di volta in volta l'osservatore verso lo scenario esterno, mentre si muove lungo il progetto, armonizzando così il panorama e la casa stessa. L'area living principale della casa è rivolta verso i bassi rami scultorei delle grandi querce in cima alla collina, angolata verso sud per la luce del sole. Gli sbalzi e i pergolati fanno da schermo al sole estivo, ma la loro dimensione consente l'ingresso alla luce invernale. Il pannello sottostante il claristorio è rivestito di vetro riflettente e getta una linea di luce sul soffitto, screziato dai giochi delle foglie in movimento, determinando la trasposizione degli elementi esterni nell'essenza profonda del progetto. La casa riecheggia l'ambiente circostante anche nel gusto dei materiali scelti.

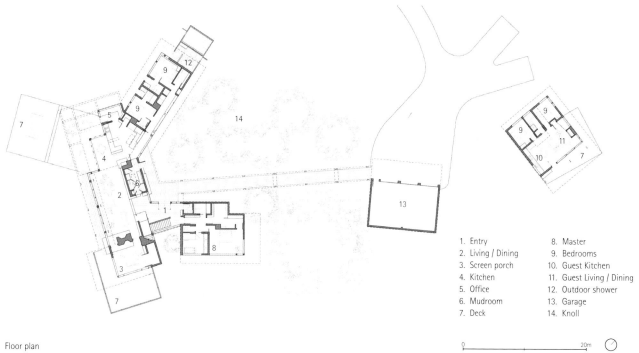

Floor plan

1. Entry
2. Living / Dining
3. Screen porch
4. Kitchen
5. Office
6. Mudroom
7. Deck

8. Master
9. Bedrooms
10. Guest Kitchen
11. Guest Living / Dining
12. Outdoor shower
13. Garage
14. Knoll

0   20m

Natrufied-Architecture designs projects in the Netherlands and abroad. With a team of international architects and designers, Natrufied is working on a broad portfolio in the areas of Live, Work, Relax, Heal and Reflect. Natrufied has been involved in a variety of commissions on all scales in the architectural field. The objective of the design firm is to be intensely involved in all stages of the projects, from first sketch until the last screw. By thorough detailing and involvement of specialist companies in early states of the projects the balance of ambitions and budget can generate maximum result of quality. The Natrufied-Architecture team combines the dynamic of a young creative office with two decades of top-level architectural experience. Combining architects as well as technical trained staff in design as well as building stages leads to maximum result.

NATRUFIED ARCHITECTURE

WWW.NATRUFIED.NL

Natrufied-Architecture conçoit des projets dans les Pays-Bas et à l'étranger. Avec son équipe d'architectes et de designers internationaux, Natrufied travaille sur un large portefeuille de possibilités dans les domaines de la Vie, du Travail, de la Détente, de l'Apaisement et de la Réflexion. Natrufied s'est impliqué dans toutes sortes de commandes de toutes proportions dans le domaine de l'architecture. L'objectif de cette société de design est de s'impliquer profondément à chaque étape du projet, du premier croquis à la dernière vis. Par le biais d'une attention minutieuse au détail, et de l'implication de compagnies spécialisées dès les premières étapes des projets, l'équilibre des ambitions et du budget peut générer un résultat de qualité optimale. L'équipe de Natrufied-Architecture associe la dynamique d'un jeune cabinet créatif avec deux décennies d'expérience architecturale de haut niveau. La collaboration d'architectes avec des employés de formation technique au niveau du design comme des étapes de construction mène à un résultat idéal.

L'attività progettuale di Natrufied-Architecture si sviluppa nei Paesi Bassi e all'estero. Con un team internazionale di architetti e designer, Natrufied lavora a un'ampia gamma di progetti nell'ottica Live, Work, Relax, Heal and Reflect (Vivi, lavora, rilassati, curati e rifletti). Natrufied è stato coinvolto in molte commissioni impegnate in tutti i campi dell'architettura. L'obiettivo dello studio di design è essere totalmente coinvolto in tutte le fasi del progetto, dal primo schizzo all'ultima vite. L'equilibrio tra ambizione e budget può generare un risultato di altissima qualità attraverso la puntuale partecipazione agli stadi preliminari dei progetti da parte di aziende specialiste nel settore. Il team di Natrufied-Architecture unisce il dinamismo di un personale giovane e creativo e due decenni di esperienza architettonica ai massimi livelli. Il risultato migliore in assoluto si ottiene con la collaborazione tra architetti e staff tecnico esperto nella progettazione nonché nelle fasi della costruzione.

ECOLOGICAL CHILDREN ACTIVITY
AND EDUCATION CENTER

 CAMPUS MARKENHAGE

NIEUW LEYDEN

At the site of the Markenhage college, the new Campus Markenhage is realized with the existing Markenhage college that got renovated and extended with an extra wing for technical education and two new schools; the new Orion Lyceum and the Michael college, a Waldorf school. Together the three schools form the new Campus Markenhage.

The Markenhage is the big mother ship in the middle of the campus with on each side one of the two new wing mates. All three schools have a façade to the main street and connected park, together they form a new cultural axis as all cultural teaching spaces of the three schools are located next to each other along the street. The Markenhage school has become a 2 level square with a patio in the middle by adding the new wing, with this the circulation of the existing building is improved so the 1000 students can find their way more easily. The new classrooms for Chemistry, Physics and Biology provide more possibilities for teaching these technical classes.

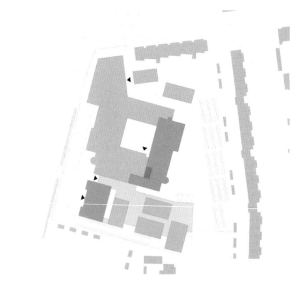

Site plan

CAMPUS MARKENHAGE

© Boris Zeisser

Sur le site du collège de Markenhage, le nouveau Campus Markenhage qui a été rénové et agrandi d'une aile supplémentaire pour l'enseignement technique et deux nouvelles écoles : le nouveau Orion Lyceum et le Michael College, une école Waldorf. Les trois écoles réunies forment le nouveau Campus Markenhage.

Le Markenhage est le grand vaisseau mère du milieu du campus avec, de chaque côté, l'un des deux seconds sous la forme des nouvelles ailes. Les trois écoles ont toutes une façade sur la rue principale et reliée au parc, et forment ensemble un axe culturel nouveau en ce que tous leurs espaces d'enseignement culturels sont situés côte-à-côte tout au long de la rue. L'école Markenhage est devenue une place à deux niveaux avec un patio en son centre par l'ajout d'une nouvelle aile, ce qui améliore la circulation du bâtiment existant afin que ses 1000 élèves puissent trouver leur chemin plus facilement. Les nouvelles salles de chimie, de physique et de biologie offrent plus de possibilités pour l'enseignement de ces cours techniques.

Nella sede del Markenhage college, è stato realizzato il nuovo Campus Markenhage rinnovando la struttura esistente ed estendendola con una nuova ala dedicata all'istruzione tecnica e due scuole:

il nuovo Orion Lyceum e il Michael college, una scuola Waldorf. Le tre scuole insieme formano il nuovo Campus Markenhage.

Il Markenhage è costituito dalla grande nave madre al centro del campus, fiancheggiata su entrambi i lati dalle nuove ali. Tutte e tre le scuole hanno una facciata che guarda sulla strada principale e sul parco annesso; insieme, esse formano un nuovo asse culturale, con gli spazi dati all'insegnamento posti uno accanto all'altro lungo la strada. La scuola Markenhage è diventata una struttura squadrata su 2 livelli, con un patio centrale derivato dall'ala di nuova costruzione. In questo modo, i 1.000 studenti che la frequentano possono orientarsi più facilmente. Le nuove classi di Chimica, Fisica e Biologia sono attrezzate in modo da favorire l'insegnamento di queste materie.

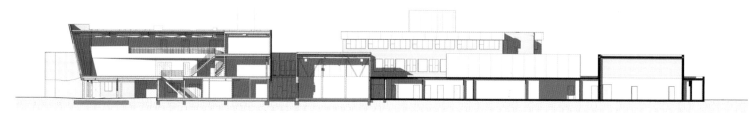

Section

The Den is located at a rocky slope close to the sea. With its Manta-ray inspired bamboo dome, perched in an elevated position so as to offer magnificent views, it seems to launch itself into the bay. The structure and roof are made from local Thai bamboo, thus contributing further to the ecological approach of the resort. The interior is made from local plantation River Red Gum wood and rattan structural elements for the inner domes.

The design adopts all bioclimatic aspects to suits its humid tropical environment. The roof cantilevers up to 8m acting like a big umbrella providing shade and protection from the heavy rains. The open design with the translucent elevated rooftop and setback floors allow a natural airflow inside and the use of natural daylight, limiting the building's energy consumption.

ECOLOGICAL CHILDREN ACTIVITY AND EDUCATION CENTER

© Boris Zeisser

Le « Den » est situé sur une côte rocheuse près de la mer. Avec son dôme de bambou inspiré de la raie manta, perché en position élevée pour offrir des vues magnifiques, il semble sur le point de se lancer dans la baie. Sa structure et sa toiture sont faits de bambou thaïlandais local, contribuant ainsi encore davantage à l'approche écologique de cette station balnéaire. L'intérieur est en bois de gommier rouge des rivières issu de plantations locales et les éléments structurels en rotin pour les dômes internes.

Le design se plie à tous les aspects bioclimatiques pour s'adapter à son environnement tropical humide. Le toit sort en saillie à hauteur de 8 mètres, faisant office de grand parapluie en procurant ombre et protection contre les fortes précipitations. Le design ouvert avec son toit-terrasse translucide et ses sols en retrait facilitent la circulation naturelle de l'air à l'intérieur et l'usage de la lumière naturelle, limitant la consommation énergétique du bâtiment.

Il Rifugio si trova su un pendio roccioso che dà sul mare. Con la sua cupola di bambù che richiama la forma di una manta, appollaiato in alto per offrire panorami magnifici, sembra volersi tuffare nella baia. Struttura e tetto sono fatti di bambù tailandese locale, un modo per accentuare ancora di più l'approccio ecologico del resort. L'interno è in legno di eucalipto rosso, mentre le cupole interne presentano elementi in rattan.

Il design tiene conto di tutti gli aspetti bioclimatici per adattarsi all'umido ambiente tropicale. Le travi a sbalzo del tetto, che misurano fino a 8 m, agiscono come un grande ombrello, offrendo ombra e protezione dalle forti piogge. Il design aperto, con l'alto tetto semitrasparente e i piani rientrati, consente una naturale circolazione dell'aria all'interno della struttura, nonché lo sfruttamento della luce solare, limitando il consumo di energia da parte dell'intera costruzione.

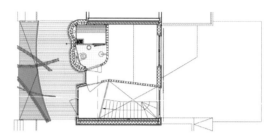
Third floor

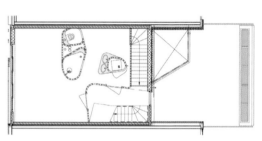
Second floor

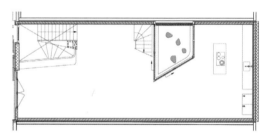
First floor

The building block consists of 18 houses, designed by different architects. There are no regulations of the beauty commission, so the future owners are free to design their house, as long as it fits within the provided building envelope.

The half sunken parking garage is situated in the centre of the building block, giving the houses a split-level arrangement, resulting in a high density area with narrow car free streets. Due the minimal amount of urban requirements regarding floor heights, shape and architectural appearance of the individual houses, the ensemble got a maximum architectural variety in shape and style, reminiscent of the historical city centre of Leiden but in a contemporary appearance.

NIEUW LEYDEN

© Boris Zeisser

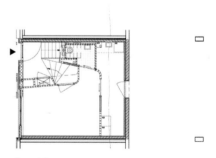
Ground floor

Cette construction est composée de 18 maisons, conçues par différents architectes. Il n'y a pas de règles esthétiques imposées, de sorte que les futurs propriétaires sont libres de concevoir leur maison, tant qu'elle contient dans l'enveloppe du bâtiment.

Le garage à voiture à moitié engagé est situé au centre de l'immeuble, donnant aux maisons une configuration sur deux niveaux, créant ainsi une zone à haute densité de population aux rues étroites sans voitures. De par le peu d'exigences relatives à l'urbanisme concernant les hauteurs de plafond, la forme et l'aspect architectural des maisons individuelles, l'ensemble est doté d'une variété architecturale maximale au niveau de la forme et du style, rappelant le centre historique de Leiden, mais avec un aspect contemporain.

Il blocco di edifici è composto da 18 case progettate da architetti diversi. Non ci sono regole alle richieste di bellezza da parte dei futuri proprietari, che sono liberi di progettare la propria casa come preferiscono, purché nei limiti dell'involucro edilizio.

Il parcheggio seminterrato è posto al centro del blocco, e dà alle case un'organizzazione su livelli separati. Il risultato è un'area ad alta densità, le cui stradine sono però prive di auto. Grazie alla quantità minima di requisiti urbanistici in materia di altezza, forma e aspetto architettonico delle case individuali, la varietà dell'insieme si esprime al massimo sia nella forma sia nello stile, ricordando il centro storico di Leida ma reinterpretandolo in chiave contemporanea.

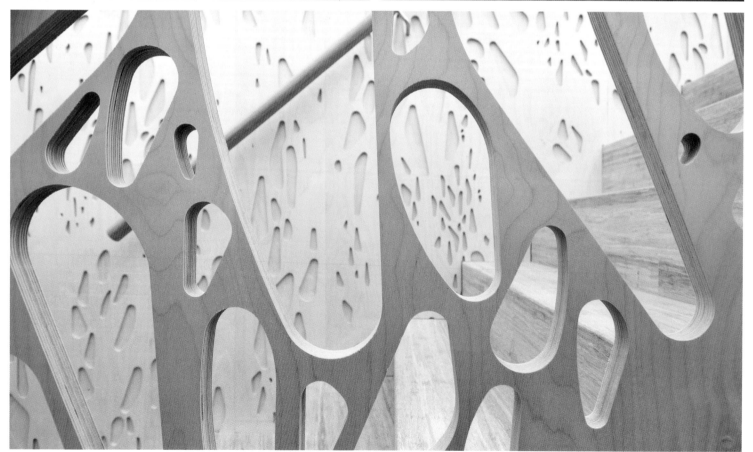

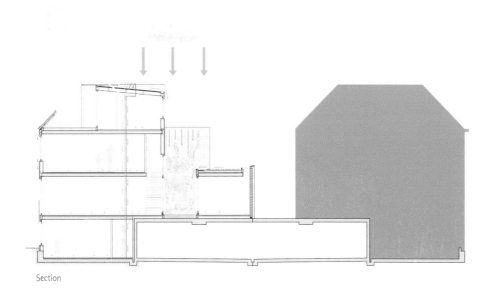

Section

Patano Studio Architecture is a practice that investigates and implements Building|Nature —our work intensifies natural experiences and naturalizes cities. Our buildings utilize locally sourced materials with specific emphasis on mass timber technologies and wood structures. High in the mountains and out in the open spaces of the west our architecture captures light and creates human scaled spaces for learning, observing and extending our curiosity into the environment and out into the cosmos. Our urban strategies are based on the city being a living organism —we are building a future where our cities are healthy, regenerative, energy generating centers for living. Patano Studio Architecture's commitment to Building|Nature drives our work forward. It all starts with our clients —our process of 'finding YES!' is the basis of all conversations, we excel at finding a way forward.

PATANO STUDIO ARCHITECTURE

WWW.PATANOSTUDIO.COM

Patano Studio Architecture est un cabinet qui recherche et met en application l'adéquation Construction/Nature – notre travail intensifie l'expérience de la nature et apporte la nature aux villes. Nos constructions utilisent des matériaux sourcés localement, avec un intérêt particulier pour les technologies du bois massif et les structures en bois. Que ce soit dans la montagne ou dans les espaces ouverts de l'ouest, notre architecture capte la lumière et crée des espaces à échelle humaine pour apprendre, observer et développer notre curiosité vers l'environnement et vers le cosmos. Nos stratégies urbaines sont basées sur l'idée de la ville en tant qu'organisme vivant – nous construisons un avenir dans lequel nos villes sont saines, régénérantes, des centres générateurs d'énergie pour la vie. L'engagement de Patano Studio Architecture envers l'adéquation Construction/Nature est un véritable moteur pour notre travail. Tout cela commence avec nos clients : notre processus de « recherche du OUI! » est à la base de toutes les conversations ; trouver la solution pour aller de l'avant, c'est notre spécialité.

Patano Studio Architecture è uno studio che ricerca e applica il concetto di Building|Nature. Il nostro lavoro intensifica l'esperienza con la natura e porta la natura nelle città. I nostri edifici utilizzano materiali di origine locale, con un'attenzione particolare alla tecnologia mass timber e alle strutture in legno. Sulle alte montagne e negli spazi aperti dell'Ovest, la nostra architettura coglie la luce e crea spazi a misura d'uomo per imparare, osservare ed estendere la nostra curiosità verso l'ambiente e, più in là, verso l'intero cosmo. Le nostre strategie urbane si basano sulla città in quanto essere vivente. Stiamo costruendo un futuro dove le nostre città siano sane, rigeneranti e funzionino a energia sostenibile. L'impegno del Patano Studio Architecture verso il concetto di Building|Nature fa da guida a tutto il nostro lavoro. Comincia tutto con i nostri clienti: il processo del 'trovare il SÌ!' sta alla base di ogni conversazione. Siamo i più bravi a trovare la via giusta.

LAKE SAMMAMISH STATE PARK BATHHOUSE
REVELEY CLASSROOM BUILDING

The Lake Sammamish Bathhouse was created in accordance with the Lake Sammamish State Park Master Plan which aims to unify the 512 acre park; integrating the building with the landscape and the landscape with the building.

The Bathhouse's structure is comprised of repetitive concrete components that have the flexibility to form a variety of enclosures and provide a durable frame that can adapt to different uses over time. The building features natural ventilation, day-lighting, planted roof, reclaimed redwood siding, low-flow/waterless plumbing fixtures and building integrated photo-voltaic (PV) panels. The PV roof panels power the building and provide educational opportunities for the park users, while allowing light to filter through to the covered outdoor spaces. Storm water is managed on-site with the green roof, rain gardens, and bio-swales to aid in the restoration and rehabilitation of existing wetlands.

LAKE SAMMAMISH
STATE PARK BATHHOUSE

© Sozinho Imagery

Le Lake Sammamish Bathhouse a été créé conformément au *Lake Sammamish State Park Master Plan*, projet visant à harmoniser ce parc de 512 acres en intégrant le bâtiment dans le paysage et le paysage avec le bâtiment.

La structure du Bathhouse est composée de la répétition d'éléments de béton qui sont assez modulables pour redéfinir une variété de périmètres et procurer un cadre durable qui peut s'adapter à différents usages au fil du temps. Ce bâtiment jouit d'une aération naturelle, de la lumière du jour, d'un toit végétalisé, d'un bardage de cèdre rouge récupéré, de matériel de plomberie à faible consommation d'eau/sans eau et de panneaux photovoltaïques intégrés à la structure. Ces derniers approvisionnent le bâtiment en électricité et offrent des opportunités pédagogiques pour les usagers du parking, tout en laissant filtrer la lumière à travers les espaces couverts extérieurs. L'eau de pluie est gérée sur site, le toit végétal, les jardins pluviaux et le système de drainage durable aidant à la restauration et à la réhabilitation des marais d'origine.

Lake Sammamish Bathhouse è stata realizzata in linea con le direttive del Lake Sammamish State Park Master Plan, che vuole unificare il parco, vasto 207 ettari circa, integrando l'edificio con il paesaggio e il paesaggio con l'edificio.

La struttura Bathhouse è composta da una sequenza di elementi in calcestruzzo disposti in modo da offrire numerosi ambienti e fornire la durabilità necessaria a rendere l'edificio adatto a usi diversi nel tempo. Caratteristiche della struttura sono la ventilazione e l'illuminazione naturali, il tetto a giardino, il rivestimento in sequoia rigenerata, gli impianti idraulici a bassa portata/senz'acqua e i pannelli fotovoltaici (PV) integrati nell'edificio. I pannelli fotovoltaici (PV) sul tetto danno energia all'edificio e offrono spunti di insegnamento agli utenti del parco; inoltre, consentono alla luce di filtrare attraverso gli spazi esterni coperti. L'acqua piovana viene gestita in loco, con il tetto verde, i giardini pluviali e le bioswale che aiutano a ripristinare e riqualificare le preesistenti zone paludose.

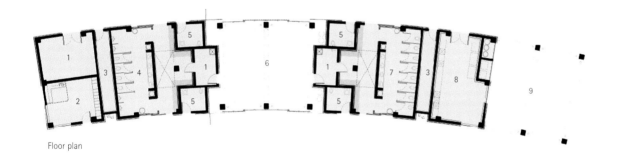

Floor plan

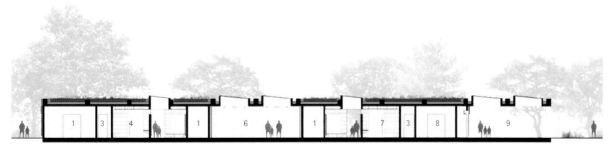

Section

1. Storage
2. Lifeguard headquarters
3. Chase
4. Men's restroom
5. Family / ADA restroom
6. Flex space
7. Women's restroom
8. Concession
9. Covered outdoor seating

In 2013, Patano Studio Architecture engaged in a unique collaboration with the University of Idaho's College of Natural Resources, to design and construct an all Idaho wood products high-performance Classroom Building at their Pitkin Nursery facility east of Moscow.

Patano Studio was chosen because of their research-based design process and experience creating high-performance building envelopes. The project utilizes Idaho Forest Products and is a working example of the variety of raw and engineered wood products that the state of Idaho produces. Additionally, the building is an international symbol for the College of Natural Resources, hosting events with partners from Spain, South Korea as well as within the state. Super insulated walls and roof and high efficiency heating result in a low-energy use building. The proper solar orientation and screening of window openings prevents unwanted solar gain.

REVELEY CLASSROOM BUILDING

© Sozinho Imagery

En 2013, Patano Studio Architecture s'est engagé dans une collaboration unique avec le *College of Natural Resources* de l'Université d'Idaho, pour concevoir et construire un bâtiment scolaire de haute performance avec uniquement des produits en bois d'Idaho dans leurs locaux de la *Pitkin Nursery* à l'est de Moscou.

Patano Studio a été choisi à cause de leur processus de design fondé sur la recherche et de leur expérience dans la création d'enveloppes de bâtiment de haute performance. Ce projet utilise des produits de la forêt d'Idaho et représente un bon exemple de la variété des produits en bois brut ou en bois transformé que produit l'État d'Idaho. De plus, le bâtiment est un symbole international pour le *College of Natural Resources*, accueillant des événements partagés avec des partenaires venant d'Espagne, de Corée du Sud ainsi que de l'État même. Des murs et une toiture extrêmement bien isolés et un chauffage à haute efficacité déterminent un bâtiment à faible consommation énergétique. L'orientation solaire appropriée et la protection des ouvertures préviennent un apport solaire indésirable.

Nel 2013, Patano Studio Architecture ha iniziato una collaborazione esclusiva con il College of Natural Resources dell'Università dell'Idaho, per progettare e realizzare un edificio di aule ad alta prestazione e interamente composto di prodotti del legno locale, presso la sede della Pitkin Nursery a est di Moscow.

Patano Studio è stato scelto per la sua tipologia di progettazione basata sulla ricerca e per l'esperienza maturata nella realizzazione di edifici ad alta prestazione. Il progetto utilizza prodotti delle foreste dell'Idaho, ed è un esempio validissimo della diversità di elementi grezzi e lavorati che lo stato ricava dai suoi legnami. Inoltre, l'edificio è un simbolo internazionale del College of Natural Resources, e ospita eventi con partner provenienti dalla Spagna e dalla Corea del Sud, oltre che dallo stesso Idaho. Muri e tetto super-isolati e impianto di riscaldamento ad alta efficienza fanno dell'opera un edificio a basso consumo energetico. L'orientamento studiato e la schermatura delle finestre impedisce l'ingresso di luce solare indesiderata.

PITKIN NURSERY
Tom & Teita Reveley Nursery Facility

C.N.R.

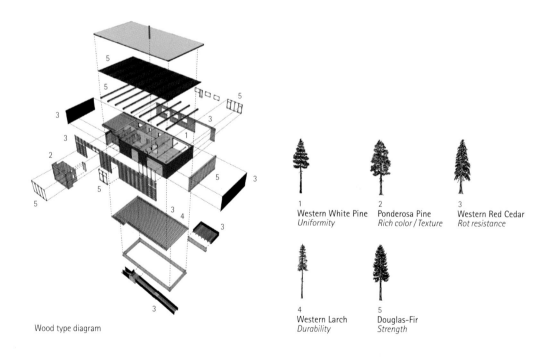

Wood type diagram

1
Western White Pine
Uniformity

2
Ponderosa Pine
Rich color / Texture

3
Western Red Cedar
Rot resistance

4
Western Larch
Durability

5
Douglas-Fir
Strength

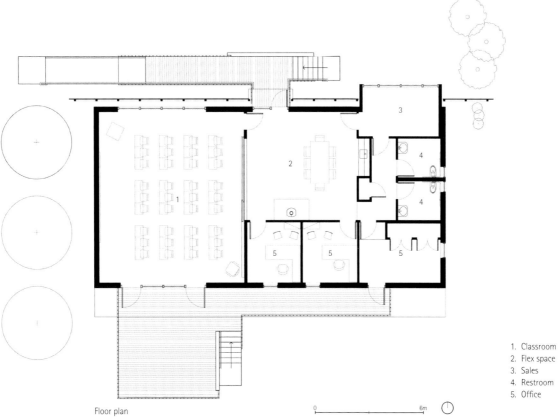

Floor plan

0   6m

1. Classroom
2. Flex space
3. Sales
4. Restroom
5. Office

North elevation

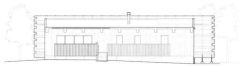

South elevation

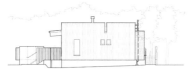

East elevation

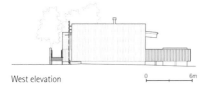

West elevation

0   6m

Plano Humano Arquitectos Atelier is an architectural atelier founded in 2008, by the architects Helena Vieira and Pedro Ferreira and is based in Lisbon, with activity in Portugal and abroad (e.g. Angola). One of the most characteristic features of Plano Humano Arquitectos has been the constant seek to explores new materials, techniques and systems in order to define buildings and spaces while exploring classical and cutting-edge technologies. The use of wood is a transversal to all projects, some of them becoming icons of the city of Lisbon, as is the case of the Lisbon Wood Building.

Recently won "The American Architecture Prize" 2017, one of the most reputable architectural awards in the world in the category Institutional Architecture, also an nomination for the Portuguese awards Prémios Construir '17 in the category of best building of the year with the project of the Pastoral Center of Moscavide, and an honorable mention in the Archizinc Trophy 2018, with the chapel project.

PLANO HUMANO ARQUITECTOS

WWW.PLANOHUMANOARQUITECTOS.COM

Plano Humano Arquitectos Atelier est un atelier d'architecture fondé en 2008 par les architectes Helena Vieira et Pedro Ferreira et basé à Lisbonne, avec activité au Portugal et à l'étranger (p. ex. en Angola). L'un des traits caractéristiques de Plano Humano Arquitectos est la volonté constante d'explorer des matériaux, des techniques et des systèmes nouveaux afin de définir des bâtiments et des espaces tout en explorant les technologies classiques et de pointe. L'utilisation du bois est transversal à tous leurs projets, certains d'entre eux étant devenus iconiques dans la ville de Lisbonne, comme le *Lisbon Wood Building*. Lauréat récent de l' *American Architecture Prize* en 2017, l'un des prix d'architecture les plus réputés du monde dans la catégorie Architecture institutionnelle, également nominé pour le prix portugais *Prémios Construir '17* dans la catégorie du meilleur bâtiment de l'année avec le projet du Centre pastoral de Moscavide, et ayant obtenu une mention honorable dans l' *Archizinc Trophy 2018*, avec le projet de la chapelle.

Plano Humano Arquitectos Atelier è un atelier di architettura fondato nel 2008 dagli architetti Helena Vieira e Pedro Ferreira, con sede a Lisbona, la cui attività si svolge in Portogallo e all'estero (es.: in Angola). Una delle caratteristiche più peculiari di Plano Humano Arquitectos è da sempre la ricerca costante di nuovi materiali, tecniche e sistemi per definire gli edifici e gli spazi ed esplorare nel contempo le tecnologie tradizionali e quelle all'avanguardia. L'impiego del legno è un punto in comune di tutti i progetti, alcuni dei quali sono diventati icone della città di Lisbona, come il Lisbon Wood Building. Lo studio ha vinto l'edizione 2017 dell'American Architecture Prize per la categoria Architettura Istituzionale, uno dei riconoscimenti più ambiti in tutto il mondo; ha inoltre guadagnato una nomination per i portoghesi Prémios Construir '17 nella categoria di migliore edificio dell'anno, con il progetto del Centro Pastorale di Moscavide, e una menzione d'onore all'Archizinc Trophy 2018, con il progetto della cappella.

CHAPEL OF NOSSA SENHORA DE FÁTIMA

The chapel is dedicated to Our Lady of Fatima and is inspired by the scouting experience: outdoor life, camping, the tent, and by the sobriety and simplicity of buildings and lifestyle. The pointy edges of the building allude to the scout's scarf, the symbol of vow and commitment of this movement. The chapel was thought out as a large tent, with open doors to everyone, at all times: a constant welcoming point for shelter, contemplation and introspection. It's very simple form, as a classical tent, is formed by a gable roof, adapted to receive all visitors. The wood and zinc structure give a simple and protective external aspect to the temple, and creates a cozy interior ambience. Inside, the covering is supported by 12 wooden beams (an allusion to the Apostles) revealing the constructive simplicity and truth. With a total length of 12m, the structure reaches its highest point at 9m, after the Altar, where the raising of the main beam increases the space depth, and highlights this sacral point.

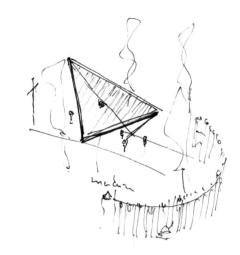

CHAPEL OF NOSSA SENHORA DE FÁTIMA

© João Morgado

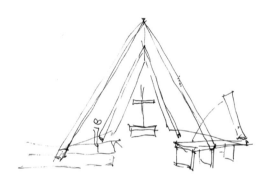

Cette chapelle est consacrée à « Notre Dame de Fatima » et s'inspire de l'expérience du scoutisme : vie en plein air, camping, tente, et de la sobriété et la simplicité de leurs bâtiments et de leur style de vie. Les arêtes pointues du bâtiment évoquent le foulard du scout, le symbole du vœu et de l'engagement dans ce mouvement. La chapelle a été conçue comme une grande tente, portes ouvertes à tous, à tous les instants : un point d'accueil constant pour trouver refuge, s'adonner à la contemplation et à l'introspection. C'est une forme très simple, comme une tente classique, formée par une toiture à deux versants, adaptée pour recevoir tous les visiteurs. La structure en bois et en zinc donne à ce temple un aspect extérieur simple et protecteur et crée une ambiance chaleureuse à l'intérieur. Là, la couverture est soutenue par 12 poutres en bois (une allusion aux apôtres), révélant la simplicité et la vérité de sa construction. D'une longueur totale de 12m., cette structure atteint son point culminant à 9m, après l'autel, là où l'élévation de la poutre principale augmente la profondeur de l'espace, et souligne ce point sacré.

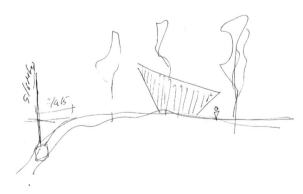

La cappella è dedicata a Nostra Signora di Fatima, e si ispira all'esperienza dello scoutismo: vita all'aperto, campeggio, tende, ma anche alla sobrietà e semplicità sia degli edifici che dello stile di vita. Gli spigoli appuntiti della costruzione vogliono richiamare il fazzolettone degli scout, simbolo di voto e impegno. La cappella è stata pensata come una grande tenda, le cui porte rimangono aperte a tutti, a qualsiasi ora: un punto di accoglienza senza interruzioni, che promuove il rifugio, la contemplazione e l'introspezione. La forma è molto semplice, una tenda classica formata da un tetto a capanna e adatta a ricevere tutti i visitatori. La struttura in legno e zinco conferisce al tempio un aspetto esterno lineare e protettivo, creando un ambiente interno intimo e accogliente. All'interno, la copertura è sostenuta da 12 travi di legno (un riferimento agli Apostoli) che rivelano la semplicità e lealtà dell'intera costruzione. Con una lunghezza totale di 12 m, la struttura raggiunge il suo punto più elevato a 9 m, dopo l'Altare, dove l'innalzarsi della trave principale aumenta la profondità dello spazio ed esalta questo luogo sacro.

Site plan

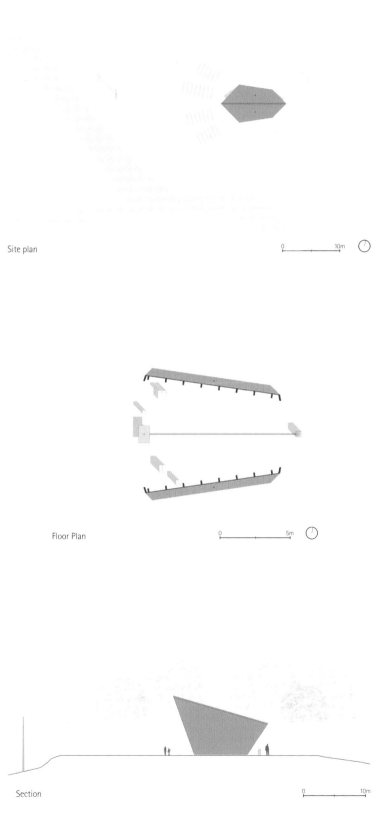

0   10m

Floor Plan

0   5m

Section

0   10m

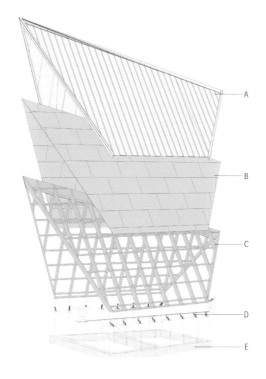

A. VMzinc plate coating, in anthra color
B. OSB board of 18mm thick
C. Glued laminated pine wood beam
D. Metal knee-cap
E. Concrete foundation

Schwember García-Huidobro is an architectural office founded in 2015 by Alvaro Schwember and Fernando García-Huidobro in Santiago de Chile. Since then, they have carried out various projects, including houses, institutional buildings, units for hydroelectric power plants and shops.
The office develops each project with special emphasis on the quality of the design, integrating aspects of sustainability and energy efficiency, providing precise and reasonable solutions for the proposals received, seeking to respect and enrich the environment. In this context, wood has played a fundamental role in its practice, being used as a construction system in several of its Works.

SCHWEMBER GARCÍA-HUIDOBRO ARQUITECTOS

WWW.SGHARQUITECTOS.CL

Schwember García-Huidobro est un bureau d'architecte créé en 2015 par Alvaro Schwember et Fernando García-Huidobro à Santiago du Chili. Dès lors, ils ont réalisé divers projets notamment des maisons, bâtiments institutionnels, locaux de machines pour centrales hydroélectriques et magasins. Le cabinet développe chaque projet en se focalisant sur la qualité de la conception, tout en intégrant des aspects de durabilité et d'efficacité énergétique, remettant ainsi des solutions précises et raisonnables pour les diverses missions confiées, à la recherche du respect et de l'enrichissement de l'environnement. Dans ce contexte, le bois a joué un rôle fondamental dans sa pratique, utilisé comme système de construction dans ses divers projets.

Schwember García-Huidobro è uno studio di architettura fondato nel 2015 a Santiago del Cile da Alvaro Schwember e Fernando García-Huidobro. Dalla sua nascita, lo studio ha realizzato numerosi progetti, tra cui case, edifici istituzionali, sale macchine di centrali idroelettriche e negozi.
Lo studio sviluppa ogni progetto ponendo un'enfasi particolare sulla qualità del disegno, integrandone gli aspetti di sostenibilità ed efficienza energetica, proponendo soluzioni puntuali e ragionevoli per i diversi incarichi ricevuti e impegnandosi a rispettare e arricchire l'ambiente circostante. In un contesto come questo, il legno gioca il ruolo fondamentale di sistema costruttivo in molti progetti dello studio.

CASA SOBRE LAS ROCAS

CASA HS

The house is located in the south of Chile, surrounded by a dense forest and large rocks from the last glaciation; in a crucial point, in a clearing of the forest to have good natural light and near to a rocky outcrop to separate from the water courses and humidity, and to gain the best views to the surroundings.

The house has been designed under the concept of refuge, like a house where the private places are of fair measures. On the other hand, the collective zones enjoy a biiger space that allows family life. The house is structured in the three axes of the Y: The north axis, corresponds to the sector of the owners, looking at a forest of oaks and ulmos. The western axis corresponds to the sector of children and guests bedrooms. The eastern axis, which corresponds to the dining room, looks at the clearing of the forest and the mountains. Finally, in the centre, where all the axes meet, there is a kitchen. Access is by a rusted steel footbridge.

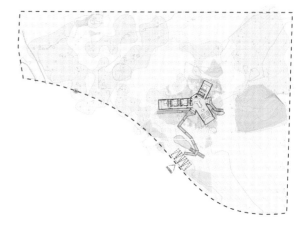

Site plan

CASA SOBRE LAS ROCAS

© Nicolás Sánchez

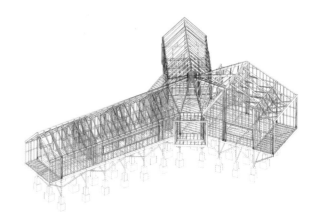

Isometric view

La maison se trouve au sud du Chili, entourée d'une forêt dense et de grands rochers datant de la dernière glaciation. La maison se trouve à un point crucial : une clairière de forêt afin de jouir d'un bon ensoleillement, sur un récif afin de s'éloigner des cours d'eau et de l'humidité, et bénéficier ainsi des meilleures vues des alentours.

La maison a été conçue selon le concept de refuge c'est-à-dire une maison dans laquelle les espaces privés sont de pleines mesures. Par contre, les espaces de vie jouissent d'une grandeur qui favoriseNT la vie de famille. La maison est structurée autour de trois axes en forme de Y : l'axe nord est réservé à l'espace des propriétaires de la maison, orienté vers une forêt de chênes et d'ulmos. L'axe ouest est consacré aux chambres des enfants et amis. L'axe est correspond au salon et à la salle à manger, orienté vers la clairière de la forêt et les montagnes. Enfin, au centre, au croisement de tous les axes, se trouve la cuisine. À l'extérieur, la maison est accessible par une passerelle en acier oxydé.

La casa è situata nella parte meridionale del Cile, circondata da un fitto bosco e grandi rocce risalenti all'ultima glaciazione. Collocata in un punto cruciale, la casa sfrutta una radura nel bosco per l'illuminazione, e un insieme di rocce per mantenersi lontana da acqua e umidità e godere al contempo dei migliori panorami offerti dai dintorni.

La casa è stata progettata secondo il concetto di rifugio, vale a dire, un luogo dove gli ambienti privati hanno la giusta misura. Viceversa, le aree collettive godono di un'ampiezza che permette lo svolgersi della vita in famiglia. La casa è strutturata come una Y, con i suoi tre bracci: Il braccio a nord è dedicato ai padroni di casa, e affaccia su un bosco di querce e olmi. Il braccio a ovest corrisponde alle camere da letto dei figli e degli ospiti. Nel braccio a est si trova la sala da pranzo, con il suo panorama sul bosco e sulle montagne. E infine, la cucina, nel punto centrale di intersezione dei tre bracci. Si accede all'esterno per mezzo di una passerella in acciaio ossidato.

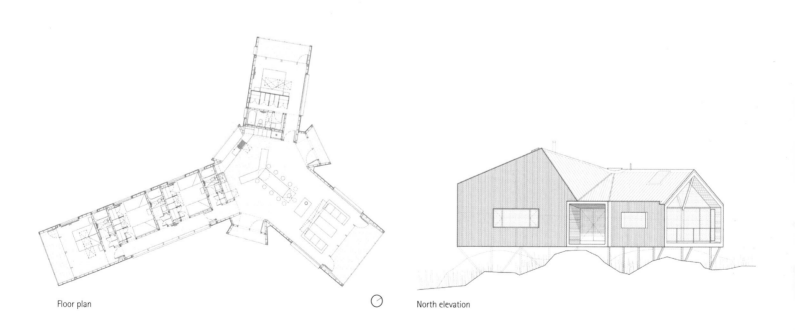

Floor plan

North elevation

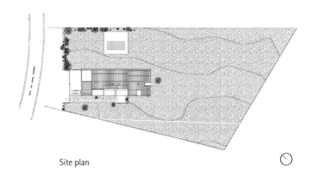

Site plan

The client asked us to design one story house, opened to the surrounded landscape where the public spaces were large in order to receive several guests.

In this way, the house was placed along the site, orienting it to the northeast, capting the best sunlight and views. Likewise, the house was divided in two areas, a public and a private one, separated and different between them, with the object to keep both zones independent. The public zone, composed by living room, dinner room and terrace, is proposed like a big continuous higher space, capable to receive large activities. Meanwhile the private zone has conventinal proportions and is closed to the family.

CASA HS

© Matucho Castillo

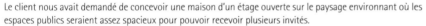

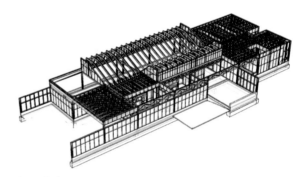

Isometric view

Le client nous avait demandé de concevoir une maison d'un étage ouverte sur le paysage environnant où les espaces publics seraient assez spacieux pour pouvoir recevoir plusieurs invités.

Ainsi, la maison a été placée dans la longueur du site, orientée vers le nord-est, pour capter le meilleur ensoleillement et les meilleures vues. De même, elle a été divisée en deux zones, une publique et une privée, séparées et différentes l'une de l'autre, avec pour objectif de les garder indépendantes. La zone publique, composée d'un séjour, d'une salle-à-manger et d'une terrasse, se présente comme un grand espace continu, capable de recevoir de larges activités. Entre-temps la zone privée a des proportions conventionnelles et elle est fermée sur la famille.

Il cliente ci ha richiesto la progettazione di una casa a un piano, aperta sul panorama circostante, con ampi spazi per la socializzazione adatti a ricevere molti ospiti.

Secondo questi desideri, la casa è stata costruita lungo l'area dedicata, e orientata verso nord-est per catturare la migliore illuminazione e il panorama più bello. Sempre secondo il volere del cliente, la casa è stata suddivisa in due aree, una pubblica e una privata, separate tra loro e diverse, ma soprattutto mantenute indipendenti l'una dall'altra. La zona pubblica, composta da soggiorno, sala da pranzo e terrazza, si propone come un grande spazio ininterrotto, adatto per le grandi riunioni sociali. Per contro, la zona privata ha proporzioni convenzionali ed è riservata alla famiglia.

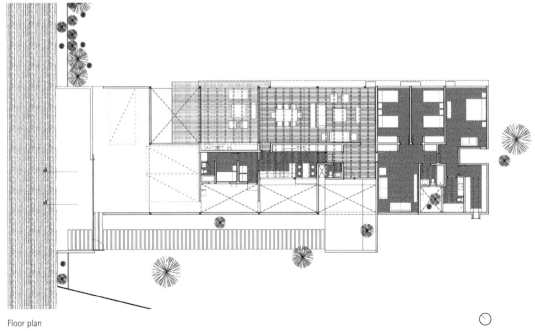

Floor plan

Based in New York City, Studio Link-Arc, LLC is an international team of architects and designers. Our name, Link-Arc, refers to the practice's collaborative nature as well as the company's mission, which is to work across disciplines to create strategy and design in the fields of urban planning, architecture, spatial art and landscape. We accomplish this by linking knowledge, resources, and intelligence, from multiple perspectives and diverse backgrounds. Our body of work includes innovative projects at all scales. We see the relationship between architecture and context as an opportunity to create new context, new nature and a new understanding of the world. Through research, we uncover the essential truths unique to each project, and use those truths to create concepts and to shape form. We endeavor to create refined works of architecture. We create spaces that promote contemplation and imagination and provide quiet satisfaction through the simple act of occupation.

STUDIO LINK-ARC

WWW.LINK-ARC.COM

Basé à New York, Studio Lik-Arc, LLC est une équipe internationale d'architectes et de designers. Notre nom fait référence à la nature collaborative de notre cabinet ainsi qu'à la mission de la société : travailler en collaboration entre toutes les disciplines pour créer stratégie et design dans les domaines de l'urbanisme, de l'architecture, de l'art spatial et du paysage. Nous atteignons cela en alliant nos savoirs, nos ressources, et nos intelligences, de perspectives multiples et de diverses provenances. Notre travail comprend des projets novateurs à toutes les échelles. Nous voyons la relation entre l'architecture et le contexte comme une opportunité de créer un nouveau contexte, une nouvelle nature et une nouvelle compréhension du monde. Par le biais de la recherche, nous trouvons les vérités essentielles qui sont uniques à chaque projet, et utilisons celles-ci pour créer des concepts et façonner des formes. Nous nous efforçons de créer des œuvres architecturales raffinées. Nous créons des espaces qui favorisent la contemplation et l'imagination et procurent une tranquille satisfaction dans la simple action d'occuper l'espace.

Con sede a New York City, Studio Link-Arc, LLC è un team internazionale di architetti e designer. Il nostro nome si riferisce alla natura collaborativa dello studio, ma anche alla missione dell'azienda: operare nel campo di discipline diverse, per creare strategie e progetti di pianificazione urbana, architettura, spatial art e paesaggio. Riusciamo nel nostro intento collegando tra loro conoscenza, risorse e intelligenza provenienti da prospettive molteplici e background diversi. La nostra opera comprende progetti innovativi su qualsiasi scala. Guardiamo al rapporto tra architettura e contesto come a un'opportunità per creare un contesto nuovo, una natura nuova e una nuova comprensione del mondo. Attraverso la ricerca, sveliamo le verità fondamentali uniche per ogni progetto, e ce ne serviamo per creare i concetti e modellare la forma. Il nostro impegno costante è la creazione di opere architettoniche perfezionate. Creiamo spazi che favoriscano la contemplazione e l'immaginazione, e che diano una quieta soddisfazione attraverso il mero atto.

CHINA PAVILION FOR EXPO MILANO 2015

Rejecting the notion of cultural pavilion as an object in a plaza, the China Pavilion is conceived as a field of spaces located beneath a floating cloud. The Pavilion embodies the project's theme, "The Land of Hope," through its unique roof form, which merges the profile of a city skyline on the building's north side with the profile of a rolling landscape on the south side, expressing that "hope" can be realized when city and nature exist in harmony. Beneath this roof, a landscaped field representing the concept of "Land," incorporates the building's exhibition program.

Designed as a freeform timber structure, the Pavilion roof uses contemporary glulam technology to create a long-span exhibition space covering a multimedia installation (the centerpiece of the Pavilion's cultural program) consisting of 22,000 LED stalks integrated into the landscape.

Site plan

CHINA PAVILION
FOR EXPO MILANO 2015

© Hufton+Crow, Sergio Grazia, Roland Halbe, Hengzhong Lv

Rejetant l'idée d'un pavillon culturel en tant qu'objet sur une place, le Pavillon de Chine est conçu comme un champ d'espaces situés sous un nuage en suspension. Ce pavillon personnifie le thème du projet, « Terre d'espoir », par sa forme de toiture unique, qui combine le profil d'un paysage urbain sur le côté nord du bâtiment avec les contours d'un décor vallonné côté sud, traduisant l'idée que « l'espoir » peut être réalisé lorsque ville et nature existent en harmonie. Sous cette canopée, un champ paysagé représentant le concept de « terre » incorpore le programme d'exposition du bâtiment.

Conçu comme une structure en bois autonome, le toit du pavillon s'appuie sur la technologie du lamellé-collé pour créer un espace d'exposition de longue portée coiffant une installation multimédia (la pièce maîtresse du programme culturel de ce pavillon) qui consiste en 22.000 brins de fibroptique LED intégrées dans le paysage.

Rifiutando la nozione di padiglione culturale in quanto oggetto in una piazza, il Padiglione Cina è concepito come spazio sovrastato da una nuvola fluttuante. Il Padiglione incarna il tema stesso del progetto "The Land of Hope," (La terra della speranza, n.d.T.) attraverso la forma unica del tetto, che fonde il profilo dello skyline cittadino visibile sul lato nord della costruzione con quello del paesaggio ondulato del lato sud, affermando che la "hope" del tema possa essere realizzata quando città e natura coesistono in armonia. Sotto questo tetto, l'area paesaggistica che vuole rappresentare il concetto di "Land" accoglie il programma espositivo della costruzione.

Progettato come struttura astratta in legno, il tetto del Padiglione sfrutta la tecnologia contemporanea del legno lamellare incollato per creare un ampio spazio espositivo che includa l'installazione multimediale (fulcro del programma culturale del Padiglione) formata da 22.000 steli LED integrati nel paesaggio.

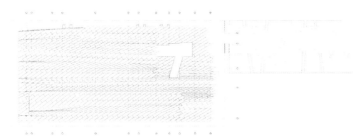

Roof plan

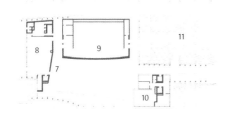

Second floor plan

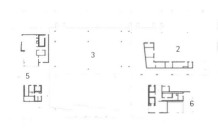

Ground floor plan

0   20m

Longitudinal section

0   20m

1. Exterior landscape   7. Panorama platform
2. Preface space   8. Banquet hall
3. Themed exhibition   9. Multimedia space
4. Led installation   10. VIP lounge
5. Restaurant   11. Bridge
6. Souvenir shop

Suzuki Makoto Atelier is based in Sapporo, Hokkaido, the northernmost part of Japan, and is a small and exclusive design office that responds to diverse client requests, such as for houses, offices and shops. All projects are designed by architect Makoto Suzuki, who cares about the fusion of simplicity and the delicate sensibility of Japanese architecture. In addition, he believes a design should not only be rational and easy to use, but also environmentally friendly and energy efficient.
Because he believes "texture" in a space leads to comfort and attachment, Makoto Suzuki takes particular care in selecting materials. A combination of solid woods, natural materials such as Japanese paper and clay walls, and hard materials such as iron and glass are among his favorites. He aims to create gentle, universal architecture that can be appreciated and enjoyed regardless of the passage of time.

© Ayu Kobayshi

SUZUKI MAKOTO ATELIER

WWW.SUZUKI-MA.COM

Suzuki Makoto Atelier est basé à Sapporo, Hokkaido, la partie la plus au nord du Japon, un petit cabinet de design exclusif qui répond à diverses demandes de clients telles que pour des maisons, des bureaux et des magasins. Tous les projets sont conçus par l'architecte Makoto Suzuki, qui s'intéresse à la fusion de la simplicité et de la sensibilité délicate de l'architecture japonaise. De plus, il croit fermement qu'un design ne devrait pas seulement être rationnel et facile d'usage, mais également bon pour l'environnement et efficace au niveau énergétique.
Parce qu'il croit que la « texture » d'un espace mène au confort et à l'attachement, Makoto Suzuki est particulièrement soigneux dans son choix de matériaux. Une association de bois massifs, de matériaux naturels comme le papier japonais et les murs en terre, et durs comme le fer et le verre font partie de ses favoris. Il vise à créer une architecture bienveillante, universelle, qui puisse être appréciée et estimée malgré le passage du temps.

Suzuki Makoto Atelier ha sede a Sapporo, Hokkaido, la parte più settentrionale del Giappone, ed è uno studio di design piccolo ed esclusivo, impegnato in progetti di varia natura, come case, uffici e negozi. Tutti i progetti sono disegnati dall'architetto Makoto Suzuki, che cura la fusione tra la semplicità e la delicata sensibilità dell'architettura giapponese. Egli crede, inoltre, che un progetto non debba soltanto essere razionale e di facile fruizione, ma anche rispettosa dell'ambiente ed efficiente dal punto di vista energetico.
L'attenzione particolare che Makoto Suzuki mette nella scelta dei materiali deriva dalla sua convinzione che la "texture" di uno spazio porti comfort e affezione. Tra i suoi preferiti, una combinazione di legni solidi, materiali naturali come carta giapponese e pareti in argilla, e materiali come ferro e vetro. Il suo obiettivo è creare un'architettura universale dai tratti gentili, che possa essere apprezzata e vissuta a dispetto del tempo che passa.

NORTH FARM STOCK
HOUSE IN TOKIWA

This plan is an extension to a factory and store that was previously designed by the architect Makoto Suzuki. The extension space involved a triangular floor plan, with emphasis given to designing a structure that would invoke a welcoming atmosphere for customers to the premises. Japanese larch was adopted as exterior materials for the shop, in order to provide contrast with the white walls of the factory. Integration of pillars with display cabinets was done to create a more charming and refined space, further contributing to a positive image of the products being sold within the customer's mind. The structure was built in Iwamizawa City, an area that experiences heavy snow. To enable the structure to withstand significant amounts of snow load, carpenters assembled a beam of white wood material at the work site (W120 × D60), consisting of ten individually stacked layers. This architecture is designed to express both the image of a traditional Japanese wooden building, while also reflecting the particular pride and care with which the company creates its home-made products.

NORTH FARM STOCK

© Graytone Photographs INC

Ce projet est une extension d'usine et de magasin qui a été conçue par l'architecte Makoto Suzuki. L'espace de l'extension comprenait un plan d'implantation triangulaire, l'accent étant mis sur la conception d'une structure qui évoquerait une atmosphère accueillante pour les clients arrivant dans les locaux. Le mélèze du Japon a été choisi comme matériau extérieur pour le magasin, pour créer un contraste avec les murs blancs de l'usine. L'intégration de piliers portant des vitrines a été faite pour créer un espace plus attrayant et raffiné, contribuant encore davantage à l'image positive des produits en vente dans l'esprit des clients. La structure a été construite à *Iwamizawa City*, une région qui est très enneigée. Pour lui permettre de supporter une charge d'enneigement significative, les charpentiers ont assemblé une poutre de bois blanc sur le site de l'atelier (L120 × P60), consistant en 10 couches individuelles superposées. Cette architecture est conçue pour exprimer l'image de la construction en bois traditionnelle japonaise tout en reflétant la fierté et le soin tout particuliers avec lesquels cette société crée ses produits faits artisanalement.

Si tratta dell'estensione di un complesso formato da stabilimento e store già progettati da Makoto Suzuki. Lo spazio aggiuntivo si è sviluppato su una planimetria triangolare, e il punto di arrivo del progetto è una struttura che crei un'atmosfera di caldo benvenuto per i visitatori dell'azienda. I materiali esterni scelti per il negozio sono in larice giapponese, per offrire un contrasto con i muri bianchi dello stabilimento. L'integrazione di pilastri e vetrine è stata scelta per creare uno spazio più attraente e raffinato, e contribuisce inoltre a imprimere nella mente dei clienti un'immagine positiva dei prodotti in vendita. La struttura si trova a Iwamizawa City, un'area colpita da forti nevicate. Per mettere la struttura nelle condizioni di resistere all'importante carico di neve, i falegnami hanno assemblato in loco una trave in legno bianco (l120 × P60), formata da dieci strati sovrapposti individualmente. Questo tipo di architettura è realizzata per esprimere l'immagine delle tradizionali costruzioni giapponesi, ma anche per riflettere l'orgoglio e la cura particolari che l'azienda mette nei propri prodotti artigianali.

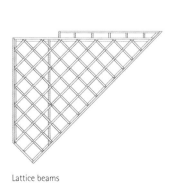

Lattice beams

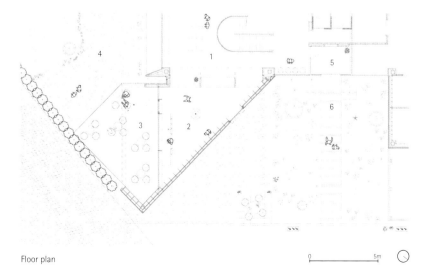

Floor plan

1. Shop
2. Extended-shop
3. Terrace
4. Garden
5. Windbreak room
6. Approach

0   5m

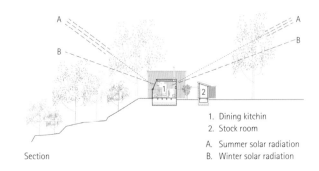

Section

House in Tokiwa is architecture that unites the architect's home and office, his wife's workplace, his father's villa, and a studio for a famous sculptor named Takenobu Igarashi through a shared space. The site is located in the outer suburbs of Sapporo, and faces a forest and river to the west side and a residential area to the east side. Japanese larch has been used on the exterior walls to suppress floor height, thus enabling the outer appearance of the structure to nestle among the pre-existing trees on the property; creating a modest appearance that blends it into the forest background. Interior floor levels, ceiling levels, and heights of apertures have been adjusted throughout the structure in order to invoke a sense that one is living deep within a forest.

In the summer, the structure is cooled by breezes emanating from the nearby river, and is protected from strong sunlight by broad-leaved hardwood trees on the east and west sides of the property. In winter, solar generated heat is acquired through the fallen leaves that surround the building.

HOUSE IN TOKIWA

© Graytone Photographs INC

La maison de Tokiwa est une œuvre architecturale qui réunit la maison et le bureau de l'architecte, le lieu de travail de sa femme, la villa de son père, et un studio pour le célèbre sculpteur dénommé Takenobu Igarashi dans un espace partagé. Le site se trouve dans la grande banlieue de Sapporo, en face d'une forêt et d'une rivière côté ouest et d'une zone résidentielle côté est. On a utilisé du mélèze japonais sur les murs extérieurs pour éliminer les hauteurs de sol, permettant ainsi à l'apparence extérieure de la structure de se fondre aux arbres préexistants de la propriété, créant un abord modeste qui le fond dans son cadre boisé. Les niveaux de sol intérieurs, les hauteurs de plafond, et les dimensions des ouvertures ont été ajustés dans toute la structure afin d'invoquer le sentiment qu'on vit au fond d'une forêt.

En été, cette structure est rafraîchie par les vents provenant de la rivière avoisinante, et elle est protégée de l'intensité des rayons du soleil par les larges feuilles des arbres des côtés est et ouest de la propriété. En hiver, la chaleur solaire est récupérée à la chute des feuilles mortes autour du bâtiment.

House in Tokiwa è architettura che riunisce la dimora e l'ufficio dell'architetto, il posto di lavoro di sua moglie, la villa del padre di lui e lo studio del celebre scultore Takenobu Igarashi, tutto in uno spazio condiviso. La zona è quella dell'estrema periferia di Sapporo, impreziosita a occidente da un fitto bosco e un fiume, e che confina a oriente con una zona residenziale. I muri esterni sono rivestiti in larice giapponese, allo scopo di mimetizzare l'altezza della costruzione e integrarla perfettamente tra gli alberi preesistenti sulla proprietà, generando un aspetto semplice che si mescola al contesto boschivo. All'interno, i pavimenti, i soffitti e l'altezza delle aperture sono stati messi a punto in tutta la struttura, per dare agli abitanti la sensazione di vivere nel cuore del bosco.

In estate, la brezza che giunge dal vicino fiume rinfresca la casa, protetta a sua volta dalla luce diretta del sole grazie alla larghe foglie degli alberi a legno duro che si trovano sui lati levante e ponente della proprietà. In inverno, il calore viene generato con l'energia solare attraverso le foglie secche che circondano la casa.

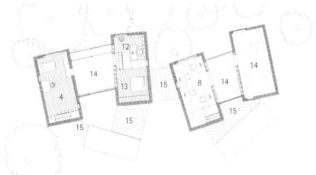

Second floor plan

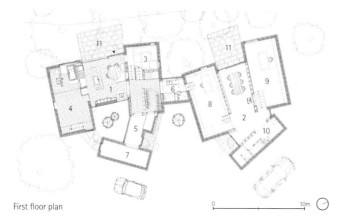

First floor plan

1. Dining Kitchin
2. Meeting space
3. Livingroom (Tatami room)
4. Weekendhouse
5. Entrance
6. Laundry
7. Stock room
8. Atelier (Architect's office)
9. Studio (Takenobu Igarashi)
10. Laundry
11. Terrace
12. Workspace
13. Bedroom
14. Void
15. Rooftop greening

0   10m

The Scarcity and Creativity Studio (SCS) is a design and build studio within the Oslo School of Architecture and Design (AHO) whose focus is on 'translations from drawing to building'. The studio's aim is to expose students to the full architectural process, from interacting with the clients to building their designs. SCS seeks challenging contexts in which local conditions and creativity are employed to make the most of scarce resources. SCS seeks proposals for projects from individuals and groups who need buildings to facilitate community activities. Christian Hermansen Cordua, Solveig Sandness, Jan Kazimierz Godzimirski.

THE SCARCITY AND CREATIVITY STUDIO (SCS)

WWW.SCS.AHO.NO

Le Scarcity and Creativity Studio (SCS) est un cabinet de design et de construction faisant partie de l'*Oslo School of Architecture and Design* (AHO) dont l'objectif principal est de « traduire le dessin en construction ». Ce studio vise à exposer les étudiants à l'intégralité du processus architectural, de l'interaction avec les clients à la construction de leurs designs. SCS recherche des contextes stimulants dans lesquels les conditions et la créativité locales sont employées pour tirer le meilleur parti de ressources limitées. SCS recherche des propositions de projets d'individus et de groupes qui ont besoin de bâtiments pour favoriser les activités communautaires. Christian Hermansen Cordua, Solveig Sandness, Jan Kazimierz Godzimirski.

Lo studio Scarcity and Creativity Studio (SCS) si occupa di progettazione ed edilizia, e ha sede all'interno della Scuola di Oslo di Architettura e Design (AHO). Il suo obiettivo è 'tradurre dal disegno all'edificio'. Lo studio vuole esporre gli studenti al processo architettonico completo, dall'interazione con i clienti fino alla realizzazione dei progetti. SCS è sempre alla ricerca di contesti stimolanti, entro i quali sia possibile utilizzare le condizioni locali e la creatività per trarre il massimo anche dalle risorse meno ricche. SCS punta a proposte di progetti che vengano da singoli professionisti o gruppi interessati a incoraggiare le attività attività comunitarie attraverso l'edilizia. Christian Hermansen Cordua, Solveig Sandness, Jan Kazimierz Godzimirski.

ECO MOYO EDUCATION CENTRE   THE BANDS   THE WAVE

Eco Moyo is a primary school located in Ezamoyo, Kenya, providing free education to children who could otherwise not afford it. SCS designed & built two classroom for Eco Moyo in the first half of 2017, and came back to build a Classroom and Study Space in the second half of 2017. Having learned that the most pleasant environment in this equatorial climate is under a large mature tree with dense shade and the uninterrupted breezes, we tried to recreate this type of space, while providing a focused learning environment and protection from tropical rain. The classroom and study space are continuous with the surrounding vegetation, with solid walls only where the attention of pupils could have been distracted by neighbouring activities. Walls: coral stone blocks, rendered in 12 parts of local red earth and 1 part cement. Structure: soft-wood and OSB frames and columns. Floors: hard-core, kifusi, DPM, steel mesh, concrete slab, steel-trowelled sand cement finish. Roof: Softwood purlins, corrugated, galvanised steel sheets.

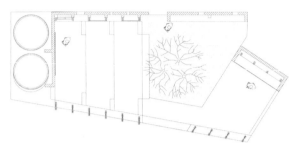

Floor plan

ECO MOYO EDUCATION CENTRE

© The Scarcity and Creativity Studio (SCS)

Eco Moyo est une école primaire située à Ezamoyo, au Kenya, procurant une éducation gratuite aux enfants qui n'auraient autrement pas les moyens d'en bénéficier. SCS a conçu et construit deux classes pour *Eco Moyo* dans la première partie de 2017, puis est retourné bâtir une salle de classe et une salle d'étude durant la deuxième partie de cette année-là. Ayant appris que l'environnement le plus agréable dans ce climat équatorial se trouve à l'ombre d'un grand arbre centenaire au feuillage dense et aux brises continues, nous avons tenté de recréer ce type d'espace, tout en apportant un environnement axé sur l'apprentissage et à l'abri de la pluie tropicale. La salle de classe et la salle d'étude sont en continuité avec la végétation environnante, des murs pleins n'étant construits qu'aux endroits où l'attention des élèves aurait pu être distraite par les activités du voisinage. Les murs : en blocs de corail, enduits d'un mélange de 12 parts de terre rouge locale et une part de ciment. La structure : cadres et colonnes en bois tendre et OSB. Les sols : hérisson, gravats (*kifusi*), film d'étanchéité, treillis d'acier, chape de béton, finition lissée à la truelle. La toiture : pannes en bois tendre, tôle ondulée et tôle galvanisée.

Eco Moyo è una scuola primaria sita in Ezamoyo, Kenya, che offre libera istruzione a quei bambini altrimenti impossibilitati a riceverla. SCS ha progettato e costruito due classi per il centro Eco Moyo nella prima metà del 2017, e una classe e uno spazio studio nella seconda metà dello stesso anno. Dopo aver compreso che il posto più piacevole, in questo clima equatoriale, è sotto un grande albero secolare, con la sua densa ombra e il venticello continuo, abbiamo cercato ri ricreare questo genere di spazio, realizzando un ambiente adatto all'istruzione, ma anche una protezione dalle piogge tropicali. La classe e lo spazio studio proseguono la vegetazione del paesaggio; gli unici muri solidi si trovano laddove l'attenzione degli studenti avrebbe potuto soffrire delle attività circostanti. Muri: blocchi di pietra corallina, interpretata da 12 parti di terra rossa locale e 1 parte di cemento. Struttura: legno dolce, assi e colonne`in OSB. Pavimenti: piano duro, kifusi, DPM, rete metallica, pannelli in calcestruzzo, finitura di sabbiacemento a frattazzo in acciaio. Tetto: Arcarecci in legno dolce, fogli di lamiera ondulata in acciaio galvanizzato.

The project was located in Kleivan, north of the Polar Circle, in a mountainous archipelago that stretches 250 kms. into the North Sea. The building was recently sold, dismantled, and re-erected on a site in Leknes Municipality. The site is on a quay containing a fisherman's cottage, a cod liver oil production building, and a cod salting building, part of a historically protected and now abandoned XIX C. which represents a form of life prevalent in this region which has ceased to exist. The three existing buildings will be renovated as to provide the accommodation for the Art and Culture Production Centre. SCS provided plans for the renovation of the existing buildings and designed and built the exterior facilities and a new sauna. The design of the building is based on three bands, each of which rises and falls independently, and in doing so both accommodates the different functions of the building and hugs the quay topography.

THE BANDS

© Jonas Aarre Sommarset

Ce projet a été implanté à Kleivan, au nord du cercle polaire, dans un archipel montagneux qui s'étend sur 250 km jusque dans la mer du Nord. Ce bâtiment a été récemment vendu, démantelé, et re-construit sur un site de la municipalité de Leknes. Ce site est sur un quai comportant une cabane de pêcheur, un bâtiment consacré à la production d'huile de foie de morue et un bâtiment pour le salage de la morue ; il fait partie d'un patrimoine du 19e siècle historiquement protégé et maintenant abandonné, qui représente un style de vie auparavant répandu dans cette région et qui n'est plus. Les trois bâtiments existants vont être rénovés pour procurer des logements pour l'*Art and Culture Production Centre*. SCS a fourni les plans pour la restauration du bâtiment d'origine et a conçu et construit les aménagements extérieurs ainsi qu'un nouveau sauna. Le design de ce bâtiment est basé sur trois bandes, chacune d'elle s'élevant ou s'abaissant indépendamment des autres, et qui ainsi accueillent les différentes fonctions du bâtiment tout en épousant la topographie de l'embarcadère.

Il progetto era stato realizzato a Kleivan, a nord del Circolo Polare, in un arcipelago montuoso che si estende per 250 km nel Mare del Nord. L'edificio è stato recentemente venduto, smantellato e ricostruito su un'area della Municipalità di Leknes. Il sito si trova su una banchina che ospita un cottage di pescatori, uno stabilimento per la produzione di olio di fegato di merluzzo e uno per la salatura del merluzzo, il tutto facente parte di un complesso storico protetto del XIX secolo, ora abbandonato, che rappresenta un modo di vivere che oggi non esiste più, ma era tipico di questa regione. I tre edifici preesistenti saranno ristrutturati per fungere da alloggi all'interno dell'Art and Culture Production Centre. SCS ha fornito i progetti per il rinnovamento degli edifici già in loco, oltre a disegnare e costruire le strutture esterne e una nuova sauna. Il progetto dell'edificio si basa su tre complessi indipendenti dal duplice scopo: soddisfare le diverse funzioni dell'opera e abbracciare la topografia della banchina.

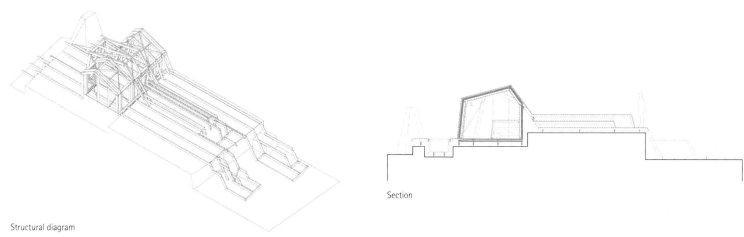

Structural diagram

Section

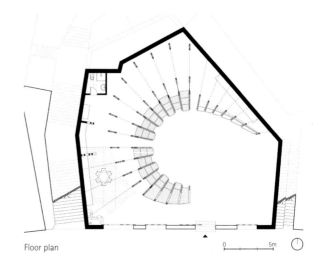

Floor plan

0   5m

Sitio Eriazo, our client, is a collective whose members recover, abandoned, derelict urban spaces in the city of Valparaiso, Chile, declared World Heritage Site by UNESCO in 2003, and put them to community use. They commissioned SCS to design and build a Public Performance Space which they use to offer free, often politically motivated, theatre, music and circus performances for the residents of the city. The design is based on a classical arena theatre. The semi-circular form serves both for seating the audience during performances and to access the upper part of the site which has a vegetable and fruit garden to supply the kitchen. The project is built almost entirely of pine softwood, the majority of which is recycled timber from other building sites. The amphitheater has now been in use for many years and has become a regular music and theatre venue in the city. The project won first prize in the 2016 Architecture of Necessity competition organized by Virserums Konsthall.

THE WAVE

© The Scarcity and Creativity Studio (SCS)

Sitio Eriazo, notre client, est un collectif dont les membres réhabilitent des espaces urbains abandonnés, désaffectés, de la ville de Valparaiso, au Chili, classée au patrimoine mondial par l'UNESCO en 2003, et les réaffectent à un usage communautaire. Ils ont commissionné SCS pour la conception et la construction d'un espace de performance publique qu'ils utilisent pour proposer des performances théâtrales, musicales et circassiennes gratuites, souvent à caractère politique, pour les résidents de là ville. Le design est basé sur l'arène de théâtre classique. La forme de demi-cercle sert à la fois pour l'assise des spectateurs durant les spectacles et pour l'accès à la partie supérieure du site qui comporte un jardin potager et un verger pour approvisionner la cuisine. Ce projet est presque intégralement construit en pin, la majorité étant du bois recyclé provenant d'autres chantiers. Cela fait déjà plusieurs années que cet amphithéâtre est en service, et il fait maintenant partie des salles permanentes de concert et de théâtre de la ville. Ce projet a gagné en 2016 le premier prix du concours *Architecture of Necessity*, organisé par *Virserums Konsthall*.

Il nostro cliente *Sitio Eriazo* è un collettivo impegnato nel recupero e nella restituzione all'uso comunitario di spazi urbani abbandonati e in rovina nella città di Valparaiso, Cile, dichiarata dall'UNESCO Patrimonio dell'Umanità nel 2003. La richiesta di Sitio Eriazo a SCS era di progettare e costruire uno spazio pubblico dato alle performance, che potesse offrire ai residenti spettacoli teatrali, musicali e circensi, spesso di matrice politica. Il progetto adotta il modello dell'arena teatrale classica. La forma semicircolare funge sia da seduta per il pubblico durante le rappresentazioni, sia da accesso alla parte superiore dell'area, dove un giardino con frutta e verdura rifornisce la cucina. Il progetto è sviluppato quasi interamente in legno dolce di pino, la maggior parte del quale è stato riciclato da altri cantieri. L'anfiteatro è ormai in uso da diversi anni, ed è diventato un luogo d'arte frequentato con regolarità dagli abitanti della città. Il progetto è stato premiato con il primo posto nell'ambito della competizione Architecture of Necessity del 2016, organizzata da Virserums Konsthall.

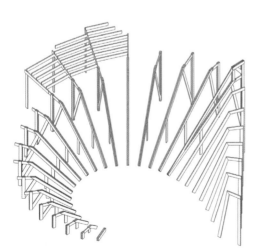

Axonometric view

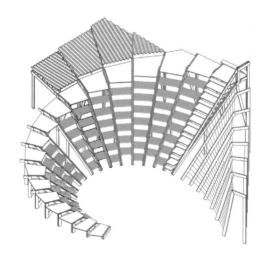

Editor of Design Media Publishing's "Urban Complex" monograph. Curator of the "Urban Dialogues, International Architecture Congress" in 2014. Winner in the 2014 Building of the Year Awards. Winner in the 2015 A+Awards. Curator of the "Mes turas, International Architecture Encounters Galicia-Portugal" in 2015, 2016 and 2017. Jury member for the DAS Awards 2016 and 2017 (Moldavia). Jury member on behalf of the Portuguese Architects Board for the João de Almada Award in 2016 and 2017. Bronze Winner in the American Architecture Prize 2016. Winner in the American Architecture Prize 2017.

TIAGO DO VALE ARCHITECTS

WWW.TIAGODOVALE.COM

Éditeur de la monographie « *Urban Complex* » de *Design Media Publishing*. Curateur de « *Urban Dialogues, International Architecture Congress* » en 2014. A remporté le prix 2014 du « *Building of the year* » et les *A+Awards* de 2015. Curateur de « *Mes turas, International Architecture Encounters Galicia-Portugal* » en 2015, 2016 et 2017. Membre du jury représentant le Conseil des architectes portugais pour le Prix João de Almada en 2016 et 2017. Médaille de Bronze de l'*American Architecture Prize* en 2016, lauréat de ce même prix en 2017.

Redattore per Design Media Publishing della monografia "Urban Complex". Curatore nel 2014 del Congresso internazionale di architettura "Urban Dialogues". Vincitore del premio Building of the Year nel 2014. Vincitore nel 2015 agli A+Awards. Curatore nel 2015, 2016 e 2017 di "Mes turas, International Architecture Encounters Galicia-Portugal". Membro della giuria in occasione dei DAS Awards 2016 e 2017 (Moldavia). Membro della giuria a nome del Consiglio Nazionale degli Architetti del Portogallo in occasione del João de Almada Award nel 2016 e 2017. Vincitore del bronzo all'American Architecture Prize 2016. Vincitore all'American Architecture Prize 2017.

THE DOVECOTE-GRANARY

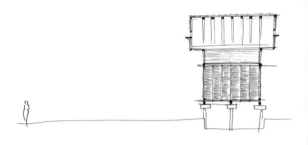

The roots of the Dovecote-Granary are humble: originally built in the late XIX century, its starting point were two traditional northern Portugal maize granaries standing over granite bases. A common roof united them under which there was a dovecote.

Built out of oak wood, the structure was under-dimensioned for the demands of that construction and, receiving no proper maintenance through an important part of its life, it rapidly decayed.

With an intricate redesign of all the subtle carpentry details and a limited set of surgical interventions that allow for its safe and renewed use, the reconstruction of the Dovecote-Granary preserves a very interesting built vernacular document, using local artisan traditional knowledge to achieve it.

Brought back as an iconic shape in the rural landscape of the Minho region, the experience of the dancing leaf shadows, the gentle crossing breeze and the birds chirping in a late summer afternoon fully defines its new purpose, function and use.

THE DOVECOTE-GRANARY

© João Morgado

Les racines du *Dovecote-Granary* sont humbles : construit à l'origine vers la fin du XIXe siècle, il a été conçu à partir de deux greniers à maïs érigés sur des bases en granit. Un toit commun les unissait abritant un colombier.

La structure, en chêne, a été surdimensionnée pour les besoins de cette construction et, sans entretien véritable durant une grande partie de son existence, elle s'est rapidement détériorée.

Avec un remaniement élaboré de tous les détails subtils de charpente et une série limitée d'interventions chirurgicales lui permettant d'être réutilisé de manière sûre, la reconstruction du *Dovecote Granary* représente un document vernaculaire conservé d'intéressante facture, s'appuyant pour ce faire sur le savoir artisanal traditionnel local.

Forme iconique rapportée au paysage rural de la région du Minho, ses nouvelles affectations et fonctions et son nouvel usage sont parfaitement caractérisés par l'expérience des ombres ondoyantes des feuilles, de la légère brise traversante et des oiseaux gazouillant à la fin d'un après-midi d'été.

Le radici di Dovecote-Granary sono umili: costruito originariamente sul finire del XIX secolo, era formato da due granai per il mais appartenenti alla tradizione del Portogallo settentrionale, che poggiavano su basi di granito. Il tetto in comune delle due strutture ospitava una colombaia sotto di esso.

Costruito in legno di quercia, l'edificio aveva dimensioni insufficienti allo scopo, e privato di un'adeguata manutenzione per gran parte della sua vita, era andato rapidamente in rovina.

Dopo la riprogettazione dei dettagli complessi e sofisticati propri della carpenteria locale, dopo un insieme di interventi strutturali volti a restituire all'uso un edificio sicuro, e attingendo dalla sapienza artigianale del posto, oggi Dovecote-Granary rappresenta un'importante testimonianza di architettura vernacolare.

La regione del Minho ospita all'interno del proprio paesaggio rurale questa forma iconica, i cui nuovi scopo, funzione e uso sono pienamente definiti dall'emozione delle ombre danzanti delle foglie, dalla brezza gentile e dal cinguettio degli uccelli in un tardo pomeriggio d'estate.

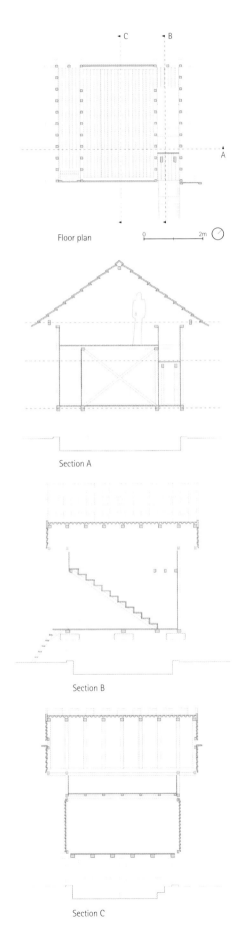

Floor plan

0   2m

Section A

Section B

Section C

We are a people-based, San Francisco, CA practice. Founded in 1998 by William S. Duff, Jr. —who leads our management team, comprised of Jim Westover, Jonathan Tsurui, Phoebe Lam and David K. Plotkin— we find inspiration in the talented people who live and work in our city and in the region's embrace of sustainability. From our location at the intersection of the city's historic manufacturing district, vibrant performing arts scene and new technology zones, our firm delivers thoughtful, innovative architecture throughout the San Francisco Bay Area and beyond. Our commitment to a culture that fosters curiosity, collaboration, and innovation drives our success in projects across our residential, retail, and commercial studios.

© GRAIL

WDA
(WILLIAM DUFF
ARCHITECTS)

WDARCH.COM

Nous sommes un cabinet axé sur les gens, basé à San Francisco, CA. Fondé en 1998 par William S. Duff, Jr – qui dirige notre équipe managériale composée de Jim Westover, de Jonathan Tsurui, de Phoebe Lam et de David K. Plotkin – nous trouvons l'inspiration chez les personnes de talent qui vivent et travaillent dans notre ville et dans l'intérêt de toute la région pour la durabilité. De notre emplacement à l'intersection du quartier industriel historique de la ville, théâtre de la vie artistique et des nouvelles zones technologiques, notre cabinet livre une architecture réfléchie, novatrice dans tout la baie de San Francisco et au-delà. Notre engagement envers une culture qui génère curiosité, collaboration et innovation est le moteur de notre succès dans des projets couverts par nos studios résidentiels, de vente et commerciaux.

Siamo uno studio di San Francisco, California, orientato alla persona. Fondato nel 1998 da William S. Duff, Jr, che guida il nostro team di gestione formato da Jim Westover, Jonathan Tsurui, Phoebe Lam e David K. Plotkin, traiamo ispirazione dalle persone di talento che vivono e lavorano nella nostra città, e dall'ottima disposizione della zona alla sostenibilità. Dalla nostra posizione, all'incrocio tra lo storico distretto manifatturiero della città, le vivaci arti performative e le nuove tecnologie, la nostra azienda realizza un'architettura innovativa e attenta in tutta la baia di San Francisco e oltre. L'impegno speso per una cultura che sostenga la curiosità, la collaborazione e l'innovazione guida il successo dei nostri progetti, dalle case, ai negozi, agli ambienti commerciali.

BIG RANCH ROAD

GOLDEN OAK

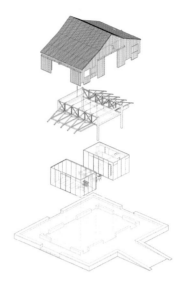

Diagram

Adventurous clients commissioned the unexpected transformation of this century-old former hay barn, an archetypal wine country form reflective of Northern California's history. Noted art patrons, philanthropists and modern architecture connoisseurs, the couple loved the wood structure's utilitarian form and sought to preserve it, while adapting the interior in a provocative way for contemporary use. The barn —made from native California redwood —was relocated without any need for demolition and sited closer to the vineyard, surrounded by site-specific artwork. The region's crisp, pure sunlight provided the catalyst for the concept —a contemplation on light. The wood-slatted shell screens sunbeams that splash ever-changing patterns on the stained concrete floors. Inside, two new opposing glass volumes whose mirrored-walls flank the gathering space reflect the barn and the surrounding environment. At night, internal illumination transforms the barn into a lantern in the landscape.

BIG RANCH ROAD

© Matthew Millman

Des clients aventureux ont commissionné la transformation inattendue de cette ancienne grange à foin du siècle dernier, forme typique de la région viticole reflétant l'histoire de la région. Ce couple, patrons des arts reconnus, philanthropes et connaisseurs d'architecture moderne, appréciait la forme utilitaire de la structure en bois et cherchaient à la préserver, tout en adaptant l'intérieur d'une façon provocante pour un usage contemporain. La grange, construite en Séquoia sempervirent, essence locale, a été déplacée sans avoir recours à des travaux de démolition et repositionnée plus près des vignes, entourée d'œuvres d'art spécifiques. La lumière vive et pure du soleil a procuré le catalyseur de ce concept : une contemplation basée sur la lumière. L'enveloppe de lattes de bois filtre les rayons du soleil qui projettent des motifs changeants sur les sols en béton teinté. A l'intérieur, deux nouveaux volumes vitrés opposés dont les murs réfléchissants garnissent l'espace principal reflètent la grange et son environnement immédiat. La nuit, l'éclairage intérieur transforme celle-ci en lanterne dans le paysage.

Dei clienti con il gusto per l'avventura hanno commissionato un'inattesa trasformazione di questo ex fienile centenario, figura archetipica della regione del vino, riflettente la storia del luogo. Nota mecenate, filantropa ed esperta di architettura moderna, la coppia è stata conquistata dalla struttura funzionale, e ha voluto preservarla adattando al contempo l'interno a un uso contemporaneo, ma in modo provocatorio. Il fienile, in legno di sequoia californiana nativa, è stato spostato senza che fosse necessaria alcuna demolizione e posizionato più vicino alla vigna, in mezzo a opere d'arte specifiche del sito. La luce naturale del posto, nitida e pura, ha fornito lo spunto per il concetto di base: una contemplazione sulla luce. Il guscio di doghe in legno fa da schermo ai raggi solari che disegnano motivi sempre diversi sul pavimento in cemento colorato. All'interno, due nuovi volumi in vetro opposti l'uno all'altro formano pareti a specchio che riflettono il fienile e l'ambiente circostante. Di notte, l'illuminazione interna trasforma il fienile in un faro incastonato nel paesaggio.

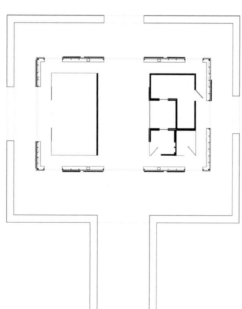

Floor plan

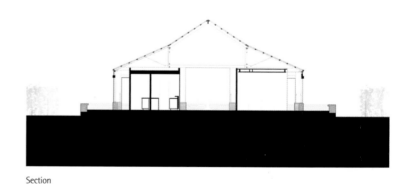

Section

Site plan

This rejuvenating family retreat was designed with two complementary wings that satisfy the clients' dual needs. Located on a hilltop in Silicon Valley's Portola Valley region, the design combines portions of an existing midcentury modern home with a substantial addition to create a unique living space. Highlighting fantastic valley views, the new butterfly roof creates a sense of openness and spaciousness that blends nicely with the surrounding property and frames the pool and pool house. The cedar-clad entry echoes the expressiveness of the roof, while offering a place of entrance and rain protection. Exposed beams on the exterior further enhance the interior architectural gestures and showcase the design's wood structural elements. In the kitchen, Koa wood cabinetry frames the white marble countertops; while, the transition between the public space, patio and pool is distinct with black metal window frames emphasizing the subtle separation between the wood and stucco exterior.

GOLDEN OAK

© Cesar Rubio

Cette résidence secondaire familiale a été conçue avec deux ailes complémentaires qui répondent aux doubles besoins des propriétaires. Situé sur une colline de la région de la vallée de Portola, dans la Silicon Valley, ce design associe des parties existantes d'une maison moderne du milieu du siècle dernier avec une imposante extension pour créer un espace de vie unique. Mettant en valeur les fantastiques vues sur la vallée, sa nouvelle toiture papillon crée un sentiment d'ouverture et d'espace qui s'accorde harmonieusement avec son environnement et encadre la piscine et la Pool House. L'entrée bardée de cèdre fait écho à l'expression du toit tout en procurant un lieu d'accès et une protection contre la pluie. À l'extérieur du bâtiment, des poutres apparentes accentuent l'écriture architecturale de l'intérieur et mettent en valeur les éléments structurels en bois du design. Dans la cuisine, des aménagements en Koa encadrent les plans de travail en marbre blanc, tandis que la transition entre les espaces communs, le patio et la piscine se manifeste par le biais de cadres de fenêtre en métal noir accentuant la séparation subtile avec l'extérieur en bois et stuc.

Questa residenza di famiglia dalle proprietà rigeneranti è stata progettata con due ali complementari rispondenti appieno alle duplici esigenze del cliente. Situata in cima a una collina nella regione di Portola Valley, Silicon Valley, il progetto combina parti di una preesistente casa moderna della metà del secolo scorso e un'importante aggiunta, per creare uno spazio abitabile dai tratti unici. Esaltando i magnifici panorami sulla valle, il nuovo tetto a farfalla crea un senso di apertura e spaziosità che ben si mescola alla proprietà circostante e incornicia la piscina e la dependance. L'ingresso rivestito in cedro riprende l'espressività del tetto, e offre un punto di entrata e protezione dalla pioggia. Le travi a vista nella parte esterna evidenziano ancora di più i gesti architettonici dell'interno e valorizzano gli elementi strutturali in legno del progetto. Il legno di Koa dei mobili da cucina incornicia i ripiani in marmo bianco, mentre la transizione tra lo spazio comune, il patio e la piscina è segnata da serramenti in metallo nero, che danno enfasi alla sottile separazione tra il legno e l'esterno di stucco.

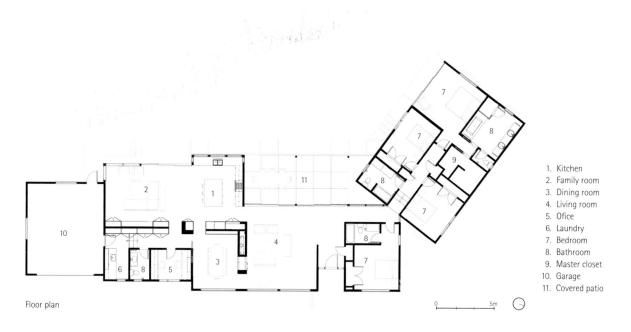

Floor plan

1. Kitchen
2. Family room
3. Dining room
4. Living room
5. Ofice
6. Laundry
7. Bedroom
8. Bathroom
9. Master closet
10. Garage
11. Covered patio

0   5m

2DM ARQUITECTOS

2 CASAS EN PUERTECILLO
Architect: Daniel Diaz M. | 2DM
Location: Puertecillo, Comuna de Navidad, Chile
Area: 118 m²
Year: 2016

CASA RAPEL
Architect: Daniel Diaz M. | 2DM
Location: El Manzano, Comuna de Las Cabras, Chile
Area: 127 m²
Year: 2016

WANKA LODGE
Architect: Daniel Diaz M. | 2DM
Location: Puertecillo, VI región, Chile
Area: 35 m²
Year: 2017

ACHTERBOSCHZANTMAN INTERNATIONAL

EE RESIDENCE
Architect: AchterboschZantman International
Location: Leeuwarden, the Netherlands
Area: 360 m²
Year: 2017

MEIJIE MOUNTAIN HOTSPRING RESORT
Architect: AchterboschZantman International, ONIX
Location: Liyang, China
Area: 6.000 m²
Year: 2015

SNEEK BRIDGE
Architect: AchterboschZantman International
Location: Sneek, the Netherlands
Area: 32 m long
Year: 2006

AIX ARKITEKTER

KATA FARM
Lead Architect: Magnus Silfverhielm.
Architect Team: Klas Eriksson, Anders Widegren, Henrik Strid, Lotta Lindgren
Location: Varnhem, Sweden
Area: 260 m²
Year: 2017

DRESSYRHALLEN
Lead Architect: Eva Göransson, AIX.
Architect Team: Eva Göransson, Lars Johansson, Katja Hillström, Martin Berg, Stina Svantesson, AIX.
Static Design: Magnus Emilsson, Limträteknik and Lars Johansson, AIX Architects
Location: Rosersberg, Sigtuna, Sweden
Area: 940 m²
Year: 2011

ANDERSSON·WISE

TOWER HOUSE
Architect Team: Arthur Andersson, Chris Wise, Kristen Heaney, Travis Greig. Structural Engineer: Duffy Engineering. Builder: Construction Arts
Location: Leander, Texas. USA
Area: 111.5 m²
Year: 2008

BUNNY RUN BOAT DOCK
Architect Team: Arthur Andersson, Chris Wise, Robin Logan, Matt Lewis. Structural Engineer: Architectural Engineers Collaborative. Civil Engineer: Aupperle Company Landscape Architect: Mark Word Design. Builder: Pilgrim Building Company
Location: Austin, Texas. USA
Area: 238 m²
Year: 2015

CABIN ON FLATHEAD LAKE
Architect Team: Arthur Andersson, Chris Wise, Jesse Coleman. Structural Engineer: Eclipse Engineering. Builder: John McCain
Location: Polson, Montana. USA
Area: 125 m²
Year: 2007

ATELIERJONES

CLT HOUSE
Architect Team: Susan Jones, FAIA; Brian Gerich; Maria Ibalucia; Joe Swain. Structural Engineer: Harriott, Valentine Engineers. Surveyor: Jouni Paavola. Geotechnical Engineer: Pan Geo. Built Green Certifier: Evergreen Certified. Passive House Consultant: Brett Holverstott. CLT Consultants: WoodWorks, ARUP. Contractor: Cascade Built LLC. CLT Fabricator: Structurlam.
Location: Seattle, Washington. USA
Area: 140 m²
Year: 2015

CLT CHURCH | BELLEVUE FIRST CONGREGATIONAL CHURCH
Architect Team: Susan Jones FAIA; Joe Swain; Michelle Kang; Brooks Brainerd; Marisol Foreman; Brett Holverstott; Megumi Migita. Owner's Rep: Trinity Real Estate. Contractor: Goudy Construction. Envelope Consultant: RDH Consulting. Structural Engineer: DCI Engineers. Civil Engineer: DCI Engineers. Acoustic Design: ARUP Engineers. Lighting Design: Blanca Lighting. Landscape Architect: Lauch Bethune. Daylighting: Integrated Design Lab. CLT fabricator: Structurlam.
Location: Bellevue, Washington. USA
Year: 2016

ATELIER OSLO

VILLA HOLTET
Architect: Atelier Oslo
Contractor: Kjetil Eriksen
Location: Oslo, Norway
Area: 214 m²
Year: 2015

HOUSE ON AN ISLAND
Architect: Atelier Oslo. Consultant: Bohlinger + Grohman Ingenieure.
Contractor: Admar
Location: Skåtøy Island, Norway
Area: 70 m²
Year: 2018

CABIN NORDERHOV
Architect: Atelier Oslo
Contractor: Byggmester Bård Bredesen
Location: Krokskogen, Norway
Area: 70 m²
Year: 2014

BFDO ARCHITECTS

20ᵀᴴ STREET TOWNHOUSE
Architect: BFDO
Location: Brooklyn, NewYork. USA
Year: 2016

SURFBOARD HOUSE
Architect: BFDO
Location: Breezy Point, Queens, New York. USA
Year: 2017

DEEP POINT HOUSE
Architect: BFDO
Location: Montross, Virginia. USA
Year: 2016

BIRDSEYE

LIFT HOUSE
Principal Architect: Brian Mac, FAIA
Project Architect: Jeff McBride, AIA
Project Team: David Kenyon, Owen Smith
Location: Killington, Vermont. USA
Area: 481 m²
Year: 2017

WOODSHED
Principal Architect: Brian Mac, FAIA
Project Manager: Rob Colbert
Area: 325 m²
Year: 2016

CARNEY LOGAN BURKE (CLB)

BUTTE RESIDENCE
Architect: Carney Logan Burke Architects
Interior Design: Tim Macdonald, Inc.
Location: Jackson, Wyoming. USA
Area: 706 m² house; 65 m² artist studio
Year: 2012

HOME RANCH WELCOME CENTER
Architect: Carney Logan Burke Architects
Exhibit Designer: The Sibbett Group
Location: Jackson, Wyoming. USA
Area: 291 m²
Year: 2013

RCR COMPOUND
Architect: Carney Logan Burke Architects
Interior Design: Dusenbury Design
Location: Montana. USA
Area: 836 m²
Year: 2016

CLARE DESIGN

DOCKLANDS LIBRARY
Concept, detailed design and interiors: Clare Design. Detailed documentation and services coordination: Hayball. Interior Fitout: Clare Design with City Design, City of Melbourne
Location: 107 Victoria Harbour Promenade, Docklands, Victoria. Australia
Area: 3.000 m²
Year: 2014

FINNE ARCHITECTS

THE DESCHUTES HOUSE
Design Principal: Nils Finne
Project Manager: Chris Hawley
Location: Bend, Oregon. USA
Area: 287 m²
Year: 2015

VENICE HOUSE
Design Principal: Nils Finne
Project Managers: Chris Hawley and Chris Graesser
Location: Los Angeles, California. USA
Area: 445 m²
Year: 2018

ELLIOTT BAY HOUSE
Design Principal: Nils Finne
Project Manager: Chris Hawley
Location: Seattle, Washington. USA
Area: 297 m²
Year: 2015

FLANSBURGH ARCHITECTS

HAWAII PREPARATORY ACADEMY ENERGY LAB
Principle-in-charge: David Croteau
Project Architect: Kelley Banks
Location: Waimea, Hawaii. USA
Area: 567 m²
Year: 2010

INDIAN MOUNTAIN SCHOOL CREATIVE ARTS CENTER
Principle-in-charge: David Croteau
Project Manager: Joe Marshall.
Project Architect: Chris Brown
Location: Lakeville, Connecticut. USA
Area: 743 m²
Year: 2013

JACOB'S PILLOW DANCE PERLES FAMILY STUDIO
Principle-in-charge: David Croteau
Project Manager: Kelley Banks.
Project Architect: Betsy Garcia
Location: Becket, Massachusetts. USA
Area: 557 m²
Year: 2017

FRANK LA RIVIÈRE, ARCHITECTS

N-HOUSE
Architect: Frank la Rivière, Architects Inc. Structural Engineers: Sato Jun Structural Engineering Office. MEP: Toho Setsubi.
Location: Aomori-ken, Owani-shi, Japan
Area: 194 m²
Year: 2007

S-HOUSE
Architect: Frank la Rivière, Architects Inc. Principal in charge: Frank la Rivière. Architect Team: Nakata Hirotaka, Kanari Ryu, Arikumi Kousuke. Structural Engineers: a.s. associates, Suzuki Aakira. MEP: Pilotis Inc, Oguma Masaharu
Location: Tsukuba-city, Japan
Area: 87.8 m²
Year: 2015

JEFF SVITAK

REDWOOD HOUSE
Architect: Jeff Svitak. Structural Engineer: Omar Mobayed
Landscape: Aron Nussbaum
Location: San Diego, California. USA
Area: 186 m²
Year: 2017

JOHN GRABLE ARCHITECTS

MUSIC BOX
Architect: John Grable Architects
Location: Sisterdale, Texas. USA
Area: 37 m²
Year: 2012

JORDANA MAISIE DESIGN STUDIO

INSTALLATION ONE: RAW ELEMENTS OF CONSTRUCTION
Architect: Jordana Maisie Design Studio. Lighting Design: Jordana Maisie Design Studio. General Contractor / Millwork: K&S Construction Renovations
Location: New York City, New York. USA
Area: 54 m²
Year: 2014

INSTALLATION TWO:
VOLUME AND VOID
Architect: Jordana Maisie Design
Studio. Lighting Design: Jordana
Maisie Design Studio. General
Contractor: Blueberry Builders.
Project Management: Prime
Design Build. CNC / Millwork:
ARC Fabrication. Flooring: Hudson
Concrete
Location: New York City, New York.
USA
Area: 39 m²
Year: 2015

KNUT HJELTNES

WEEKEND HOUSE HANSEN/
LINDSTAD
Architect: Knut Hjeltnes
sivilarkitekter MNAL AS. Project
architects: Knut Hjeltnes (pl), Nils
Joneid, Sieglinde Muribø, Øystein
Trondahl, Jens Høklid Arnolden (stud
arch.). Structural engineer: Solveig
Sandness. Builder: Petter Henriksen.
Wood structure: Porsanger
Treindustri AS. Windows and glass:
Nordvestvinduet AS. Furnishings and
stairs: Porsanger Treindustri AS
Location: Gravningsund, Nordre
Sandøy, South Eastern Norway
Area: 68.6 m²
Year: 2014

WEEKEND HOUSE STRAUME,
SILDEGARNSHOLMEN
Architect: Knut Hjeltnes
sivilarkitekter MNAL AS. Project
architects: Knut Hjeltnes (pl), Tora
Arctander, Nils Joneid, Sieglinde
Muribø, Hans-Kristian Hagen,
Maria Nesvaag (model). Structural
engineer: Siv.ing. Finn-Erik Nilsen AS.
Builder: Handverksbygg AS. Steel:
Hasund Mekaniske Verksted AS.
Windows and glass: Nordvestvinduet
AS. Furnishings and stairs: CKI AS /
AM Entreprenør AS
Location: Sildegarnsholmen, Herøy,
Western Norway
Area: 149.5 m²
Year: 2016

LANDAU + KINDELBACHER

HOUSE BY THE LAKE
Architect: Landau + Kindelbacher
Year: 2016

LUKKAROINEN ARCHITECTS

PUDASJÄRVI LOG CAMPUS
Architect team: Pekka Lukkaroinen,
Kristian Järvi, Timo Leiviskä, Hannu
Tuomela
Location: Pudasjärvi, Finland
Area: 9,778 m²
Year: 2016

LUND HAGEM ARKITEKTER

CABIN KVITFJELL
Architect: Lund Hagem Arkitekter
Location: Kvitfjell - Ringebu. Norway
Area: Gross areas: main cabin,
approx. 120 m² + annex, approx. 30
m² + carport
Year: 2016

LILLE ARØYA
Architect: Lund Hagem Arkitekter
Location: Larvik. Norway
Area: 75 m²
Year: 2014

MARLENE ULDSCHMIDT

THE PAVILLION
Architect: Marlene Uldschmidt.
Collaborators: Sara Glória, Architect;
Alexandra Jacinto, Architect.
Carpentry: Equipa Quatro Comércio e
Construções, Lda.
Location: Algarve, Portugal
Area: 21 m²
Year: 2015

MARYANN THOMPSON
ARCHITECTS

THE OAKS
Architect: Maryann Thompson
Architects
Location: Martha's Vineyard,
Massachusetts. USA
Area: 427 m²

NATRUFIED ARCHITECTURE

CAMPUS MARKENHAGE
Architect: Boris Zeisser
Location: Breda, the Netherlands
Year: 2017

ECOLOGICAL CHILDREN ACTIVITY
AND EDUCATION CENTER
Architect: 24H > architecture.
Design: Boris Zeisser, Maartje
Lammers with Olav Bruin, Anne
Laure Nolen. Bamboo consultant:
Jörg Stamm, Colombia. Local
architect: Habita architects, Thailand.
Structural engineer building:
Planning & Design, Thailand.
Structural engineer for windtunnel
tests: Ove Arup Thailand
Location: Koh Kood, Thailand
Area: 165 m²
Year: 2009

NIEUW LEYDEN
Architect: 24H > architecture.
Design: Maartje Lammers, Boris
Zeisser with Olav Bruin, Anja
Verdonk, Albert-Jan Vermeulen, Yana
Vlasova, Floor Kokke, Valentine van
Dam
Location: Leiden, the Netherlands
Area: 200 m²
Year: 2011

PATANO STUDIO ARCHITECTURE

LAKE SAMMAMISH
STATE PARK BATHHOUSE
Architect: Patano Studio
Architecture. Landscape Architect:
RW Droll Landscape Architecture.
Structural Engineer: KPFF. Civil
Engineer: MC2. Mechanical Engineer:
Rainbow Consulting. Electrical
Engineer: Coffman Engineers.
Environmental Engineer: The
Watershed Company. Contractor: A-1
Landscaping and Contracting
Location: Issaquah, Washington. USA
Area: 504 m²
Year: 2015

REVELEY CLASSROOM BUILDING
Architect: Patano Studio
Architecture. Structural Engineer:
DCI Engineers.
Civil Engineer: Tate Engineering.
Mechanical Engineer: Energy Control,
Inc. Electrical Engineer: Eidam &
Associates. Contractor: Quality
Contractors LLC
Location: Moscow, Idaho. USA
Area: 198 m²
Year: 2014

PLANO HUMANO ARQUITECTOS

CHAPEL OF NOSSA SENHORA
DE FÁTIMA
Architects: Plano Humano
Arquitectos - Pedro Ferreira and
Helena Vieira, arch. Design Team:
Pedro Ferreira, Helena Vieira, João
Martins. Engineering: Tisem -
Emanuel Lopes; IdeaWood - Amilcar
Rodrigues; Gaplr – Luis Reis,
Hermano Henriques.
Builder: IdeaWood
Location: National Scouts Activities
Camp, Idanha-a-Nova, Portugal
Area: 100 m²
Year: 2017

SCHWEMBER GARCÍA-
HUIDOBRO ARQUITECTOS

CASA SOBRE LAS ROCAS
Architects: Álvaro Schwember,
Fernando García-Huidobro. Cálculo
estructural: Patricio Bertholet. Kit
Prefabricado de madera: Playgood.
Construcción: San Manuel
Location: Lipulli, Lago Colico, IX
región, Chile
Area: 207 m²
Year: 2017

CASA HS
Architects: Álvaro Schwember,
Fernando García-Huidobro. Cálculo
estructural: Patricio Bertholet. Kit
Prefabricado de madera: Playgood.
Construcción: Dreco
Location: Condominio Los Algarrobos
IV, Chicureo, Colina, Región
Metropolitana, Chile
Area: 267 m²
Year: 2017

STUDIO LINK-ARC

CHINA PAVILION
FOR EXPO MILANO 2015
Architects: Tsinghua University +
Studio Link-Arc. Chief Architect:
Yichen Lu. Project Manager:
Kenneth Namkung, Qinwen Cai.
Project Team: Hyunjoo Lee, Dongyul
Kim, Yoko Fujita, Alban Denic,
Shuning Fan, Mario Bastianelli,
Ivi Diamantopoulou, Wei Huang,
Zachary Grzybowski, Elvira Hoxha,
Aymar Mariño-Maza, Zhou Yuan,
Chen Hu. Architect and Engineer of
Record: F&M Ingegneria. Structural
Engineer: Simpson Gumpertz &
Heger + F&M Ingegneria. Enclosure
Engineer: Elite Facade Consultants +
ATLV. MEP Engineer: F&M Ingegneria
+ Beijing Qingshang Environmental
Art & Architectural Design
Location: Milano, Italy
Area: 4,590 m²
Year: 2015

SUZUKI MAKOTO ATELIER

NORTH FARM STOCK
Architect: Makoto Suzuki.
Engineering: Yamawaki Katsuhiko
Architectural Engineering Design.
Builder: Takebe Kensetsu Co. Ltd.
Location: Iwamizawa Hokkaido Japan
Area: 54 m²
Year: 2016

HOUSE IN TOKIWA
Architect: Makoto Suzuki.
Engineering: Den Koubou. Builder:
Owl Loghomes
Location: Sapporo Hokkaido Japan
Area: 240 m²
Year: 2015

THE SCARCITY
AND CREATIVITY STUDIO (SCS)

ECO MOYO EDUCATION CENTRE
Architect: The Scarcity and Creativity
Studio (SCS)
Location: Ezamoyo, Kenya
Area: 100 m²
Year: 2017

THE BANDS
Architect: The Scarcity and Creativity
Studio (SCS)
Location: Kleivan, Lofoten, Norway
Area: 90 m²
Year: 2015

THE WAVE
Architect: The Scarcity and Creativity
Studio (SCS)
Location: Valparaíso, Chile
Area: 250 m²
Year: 2015

TIAGO DO VALE ARCHITECTS

THE DOVECOTE-GRANARY
Architect team: Tiago do Vale, María
Cainzos Osinde. Collaborators: Maria
João Araújo, Camille Martin, Eva
Amor, Hugo Quintela. Construction:
José Amorim Lima, Lda
Location: Ponte de Lima, Portugal
Area: 42 m²
Year: 2017

WDA (WILLIAM DUFF
ARCHITECTS)

BIG RANCH ROAD
Architect: WDA (William Duff
Architects). General Contractor:
Centric. Structural Engineer: GFDS
Engineers. Lighting Designer: Eric
Johnson. Landscape Architect: Steve
Arns
Location: Napa, California. USA
Year: 2014

GOLDEN OAK
Architect: WDA (William Duff
Architects). General Contractor:
Jim Dailey Construction. Structural
Engineer: Holmes Structures
Location: Portola Valley, California.
USA
Year: 2013